the
cocktail
parlor

the cocktail parlor

how women brought the cocktail home

Nicola Nice

Foreword by Robert Simonson
Cover Art and Illustrations by T.J. River

Countryman Press

An Imprint of W. W. Norton & Company
Independent Publishers Since 1923

For information about permission to reproduce selections from this book, write to
Permissions, Countryman Press, 500 Fifth Avenue, New York, NY 10110

For information about special discounts for bulk purchases, please contact
W. W. Norton Special Sales at specialsales@wwnorton.com or 800-233-4830

Manufacturing by Versa Press
Book design by Allison Chi
Production manager: Devon Zahn

Countryman Press
www.countrymanpress.com

An imprint of W. W. Norton & Company, Inc.
500 Fifth Avenue, New York, NY 10110
www.wwnorton.com

978-1-68268-871-7

10 9 8 7 6 5 4 3 2 1

For Ladybug, who loved a cozy parlor.

"Cheers to the hostess, whose welcome is most cordial.
And whose cordial is most welcome."

CONTENTS

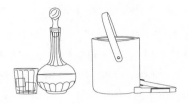

FOREWORD

If you study and write about something long enough, as I have with bars and cocktails, you begin to think you know the subject backward and forward—or, at least, the history that is known.

But blind spots are always possible. And you never notice them until someone else points them out, because, well, they're blind spots. I learned this a few years ago, when a liquor company asked me to tally what I thought were the most influential cocktail books of all time. It was free content for the brand's Instagram page, so I tossed off the list of nine books, published between 1862 and 2017, without much thought. I didn't expect much feedback, but one commenter, a marketer turned distiller named Dr. Nicola Nice, was not pleased. "Wow, not a single book authored by a woman?!" she wrote. "Shame when there are so many . . ."

OK. I responded by asking who she would have included on the list. For I was at a loss. Opportunities for women to write cocktail books and bar manuals in the 19th and early 20th centuries—the period from whence most important bar books hail—were about as common as chances for women to tend bar. The books just weren't there.

Dr. Nice then rattled off a list of writers I had either never heard of or not seriously considered. They were not the authors of bartending guides, but of manuals devoted to housekeeping, etiquette, and entertaining, the sort published with the woman reader in mind. I had seen copies of some of the titles in my cocktail history research, but had passed them over, thinking they didn't apply to my field of inquiry. I was wrong.

The simple, yet profound, truth that Dr. Nice has uncovered in her survey of hospitality guides and cookbooks penned by women—the truth expressed in these pages—is that homemakers had as much to do with the spread of cocktail culture as the saloon keepers did. The books we cocktail historians have lionized, volumes by revered figures like Jerry Thomas and Harry Johnson, were written by bartenders and were intended for bartenders. Their scope of influence was the barroom and, therefore, limited.

But, beginning in the late 19th century, people began to drink cocktails at home as well. It certainly wasn't bartenders who were preparing and serving those drinks. It was the wives and daughters and hostesses whose realm was the home and who were responsible for making sure their partners and guests had the refreshments they desired. And, like bartenders, these women were in charge of setting the scene and striking the correct atmosphere, one conducive to pleasurable imbibing and socializing.

Since much of the cocktail drinking in the world occurs in the home, these domestic efforts were not of small account. Dr. Nice's words here, as well as those found in the many volumes by woman authors that she has collected over the years, make a strong case for the role of the hostess in the explosive popularity of the cocktail over the last century and a half.

So, let's raise a toast to this illuminating book, which covers an unexplored chapter in the cocktail's long story. (If you're not sure how to properly make a toast, the good Doctor, following in the footsteps of the writers she celebrates, has mapped out the steps for you at the end of this book.) And, while we're at it, one more toast to the history you don't know.

—*Robert Simonson*

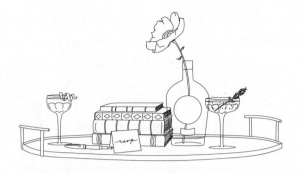

WELCOME TO THE COCKTAIL PARLOR

*Something on a Tray in front of the Fire: Chesterfield. Lovely
Cushions. Room full of Flowers. New Novel. Box of Chocolates.
Warm and becoming Negligée. Blazing Fire. Cigarettes.*
—ROSE HENNIKER HEATON, 1931

Come for a cocktail! But where shall we toast? Is there a place in your house where you most enjoy sipping a drink?

Two-thirds of our cocktail consumption happens at home, and while most of us don't have a room in our house with a sign on the door that says "Bar," there is usually a place in every home that makes the perfect spot for a cocktail. It's very easy to recognize because it's usually the place that most exudes the personality of its host. I call this place the Cocktail Parlor.

The origin of the English word *parlor* (or as my British parents would insist, *parlour*), derives from the French verb *parler*, meaning "to speak" or "to converse." During the 18th century in America, the parlor was the room in the house where a family would formally receive its visitors. Back in the day, having a parlor in your home was a sign of a family's wealth and social status. The most decorative furniture and expensive works of art a family owned would usually be on display in the parlor, and it was a space where anyone who visited—including the hosts themselves—would be on their best behavior.

It was the lady of the house who was responsible for designing the parlor, and she also took charge of its daily upkeep. In the early 19th century, visitors to the parlor would often be greeted by the hostess with a special drink made by her, such as a homemade cordial or punch. The parlor was also the room where the family would gather during the evening or on a Sunday to participate in quiet activities like reading and sewing or more social ones like performing music and playing parlor games.

As houses grew bigger through the 19th century, some of these activities moved to other rooms in the house. The front parlor became more of a waiting room near the home's front entrance where visitors would be formally received in the daytime. In the evening, dinner guests were more likely to be welcomed into the inner sanctum of the home, the *drawing room*, where they would be greeted by the hosts before being escorted into the dining room. Both guests and hosts would then *withdraw* to that room again after dinner to take their coffee and liqueurs. In some houses, a third parlor, the *lady's parlor*, was a cozy retreat near the lady's bedroom where she might entertain a group of her closest female friends over a pot of tea, or perhaps even a pitcher of wine cup.

After the First World War, the formality of the front parlor was pushed aside in favor of the family *living room*. This was designed to be a comfortable room where both family and visitors could come together in an atmosphere that was lighter, more intimate, and altogether more relaxed. The living room would come into its own during the Prohibition years as the setting for the first-ever cocktail parties and would continue to be the main venue of choice for the cocktail party throughout the midcentury.

By the second half of the 20th century, the desire to bring all social activities into one space—not only drinking and socializing, but cooking and eating as well—led architects to design houses with a more open floorplan. In North America, the *great room* concept was inspired by the great halls of medieval Europe, where the kitchen was planned at the heart of a multiroom expanse incorporating the family room, dining room, and often a parlorlike front reception area as well. This enabled more flexible hosting using the kitchen island as a focal point enabling the preparation by the hostess, for example, of a few pitcher drinks or frozen cocktails.

While the architecture and design of our spaces for entertaining may have changed over the years, many of our customs of hosting have remained remarkably consistent. Today, the Cocktail Parlor may no longer be a formal reception room or a basement speakeasy with a built-in bar. It may not even be an entire room. In many homes, the perfect place for a cocktail could be as simple as two chairs on the back porch, a loveseat in the front window, or an old leather wingback chair by the fire. The feeling evoked by this space, however, is universal. The Cocktail Parlor is the place where home hospitality, expressed through the act of the cocktail, is most cordially offered and received.

THE HOSTESS IN THE PARLOR

Interior designer and cocktail lover Elsie de Wolfe once famously wrote, "It is the personality of the mistress that the home expresses. Men are forever guests in our homes, no matter how much happiness they may find there." The reverse could be said, however, when it comes to the bar—a place where, for almost two centuries, women had to be accompanied by men, if they were even allowed in at all.

Yet despite the fact that the large majority of our cocktails are consumed at home, the history of the cocktail is rarely told from the perspective of the home Cocktail Parlor, or from the point of view of its hostess. There has always been a prevailing assumption that most cocktails started out in bars and only became established in the canon of home cocktail culture once bartenders—usually men—had documented them in bartending guides. Very few historians have stopped to ask the obvious question: what might women have written about drinks?

About 10 years ago, I started out on a very personal journey to answer this question for myself. As someone who loves hospitality and cocktails at night and who is a commercial sociologist studying beverage trends and drinking cultures by day, I wanted to understand where the conventions and norms of the cocktail had originated. I had a sneaking suspicion that as the chief entertainers of the home for centuries, women may have had something to say about the cocktail. And so, I began collecting every book I could find over the life of the cocktail that (a) was written by a woman, and (b) openly discussed mixed alcoholic beverages on the assumption that it could have served as a resource for our mothers, grandmothers, and great-grandmothers when they were looking for inspiration on the cocktail. The books I collected included cookbooks, household management guides, entertaining handbooks, etiquette manuals, and lifestyle guides from around 1800 to the present day.

What started as a handful of books soon became a library, and what started as a hobby soon became a mission. I very quickly realized that it wasn't simply that women had been overlooked in the story of the cocktail, it was that the very story of the cocktail itself was not even halfway told. The books provided all the evidence I needed to show that women have not only written about cocktails and served them in their parlors but, in the sheer volume of books they have produced, have likely had a profound influence on the cocktails served by millions of other women (and men) worldwide. What is more, many of the drinks that have found their way into wider drinking culture over the last two centuries have most likely done so because women, or rather, hostesses, have brought them home.

This book is my attempt to tell the story of cocktails through the words of around 100 women who have written about them. I have documented the works of these women as a reference in the bibliography at the back of this book. I believe such a resource to be the first of its kind. It's not an exhaustive list, but it's a starting place for any future hosts or hostesses to look for inspiration for their own Cocktail Parlors.

THE COCKTAILS

On average, most of us probably have around three signature cocktails that are the go-to drinks on our home menu. Of course, we will sometimes experiment with new recipes, or rotate a few of our favorites in and out seasonally, but for the most part we know what we like. Having a cocktail is a highly ritualistic act, and as with any transitional ritual, consistency and familiarity are key.

For a cocktail to secure its place on a host's home menu, it usually has to fulfill three basic criteria. First, it has to taste good. That goes without saying. This must be a drink that we crave as soon as the sun goes down, or whenever it's five o'clock somewhere. Second, it has to be easy to make. In general, if a cocktail takes more than two major steps or has more than three principal ingredients (not counting ice and garnish), it frankly starts to feel like more of a chore than it does a simple ceremony. And third, the ingredients must always be accessible and close at hand. If even the simplest new recipe requires some obscure or hard-to-find ingredient, the chances are that for most of us, it will not make it onto our everyday home menu.

Notwithstanding the odd regional variation, statistics show that the top five cocktails made in the United States today are the Margarita, Martini, Mimosa, Old-Fashioned, and Moscow Mule. Around 100 years ago, these would have been the Martini, Manhattan, Old-Fashioned, Whiskey Highball, and Whiskey Sour. And just about 100 years before that, it would likely have been Punch, Roman Punch, Mint Julep, Sherry Cobbler, and Cup.

Home recipe books over the last two centuries reveal a clear picture of what we have been serving in the home from one generation to the next. Over the next 10 chapters, we will go on a journey into the cocktail from the kitchens of the early 19th-century domestic hostesses to the tea parlors of the early 20th-century tea party hostess; from the apartments of single women in the late 20th century to the bars of contemporary craft mixologists in the early 21st century. Along the way, we will sip such drinks as Victorian Sherry Cobblers, Prohibition-era Bee's Knees, 1990s 'Tinis, and modern crafted Negronis; and we will discover how generations of hostesses have helped shape these cocktails into what they are today. Alongside hosting history, we will also see how cocktail history has been influenced by successive waves of feminism and women's fight for our rights *outside* the home.

With each chapter, we will meet a different set of hostesses, each writing for a different generation and segment of society, whose tips on entertaining and drinks are surely as relevant to the hosts and hostesses of today as they were many decades ago. At the end of each chapter, we will share the recipes that defined their generation and continue to have a place on modern home menus. And in the final chapter, we will come full circle, exploring the important topic of *not* drinking alcohol (with recipes for no-proof cocktails) and what it has meant, throughout the years, to be a responsible hostess.

With every hosting period, there follows a group of recipes that fall into a distinct genre of cocktail. However, this is not with the intention of trying to tie specific drinks to one type of person or period in time; rather, to suggest an easy reference for how different styles of cocktail might fit into a certain style of hosting and categories of drink in the home today.

None of the recipes—with the exception of those in the final chapter—is original or is claimed as such. These are classic recipes that have been adapted from those written in hosting books at a specific moment in time. As we shall see, customization and personalization of popular recipes have been features of the way hostesses have served cocktails across the generations. Therefore, each recipe should be thought of as a template that can be adjusted to suit personal tastes, flavor preferences, season, or just for fun. Scores of classic variations that work within the same template are also shared, as are suggestions for how to personalize each drink with simple flavor ideas.

GETTING STARTED

THE BAR CART

To make the totality of cocktails in this book you would need to keep a fairly large selection of spirits on your bar, including:

+ Brown spirits—bourbon, rye, Scotch whisky, dark rum, cognac, brandy
+ White spirits—gin, vodka, blanco tequila, white rum, mezcal
+ Liqueurs—Curaçao, triple sec, amaro, coffee liqueur, various fruit and herbal liqueurs

However, with a well-curated six-bottle bar, you should be able to make most of the recipes in this book that appeal to you specifically. This is because for almost every recipe featured there is at least one variation using the same or similar template with a different spirit base or other flavor.

For a six-bottle bar, I suggest starting with the basics: to include two types of brown spirit, two types of white spirit, and two types of liqueur. For me, the bottles I most likely reach for on my bar cart are bourbon, rye, gin, blanco tequila, Curaçao, and amaro. These bottles might be slightly different for you, but in the interests of economy and simplicity, six bottles is a good place to start.

Next to the six chosen bottles on your bar cart, you should have your standard barware kit, which will include a cocktail shaker, mixing glass, jigger, long spoon, small paring knife, and multipurpose strainer. I'm assuming that most people already know what these are and how to use them, since they are universal tools for the home bar these days, but of course easy mixing instructions are included with every recipe.

THE COCKTAIL PANTRY

Your cocktail pantry is where you will keep all of your cocktail seasonings and mixers. For a full complement that would cover almost all of the recipes in this book these would include:

+ Aromatized and fortified wines—dry white vermouth, sweet red vermouth, sherry
+ Wine—Champagne, red wine, white wine
+ Bitters—aromatic bitters, orange bitters
+ Garnishes—cocktail olives, onions, maraschino cherries
+ Citruses—lemon, lime, orange, grapefruit
+ Fresh fruits and herbs—strawberries, raspberries, mint, cucumber, pineapple
+ Homemade cordials—simple syrup, raspberry syrup, lemon cordial, cherry shrub
+ Mixers—club soda, tonic, ginger beer, ginger ale, cola, pineapple juice, tomato juice, cranberry juice, cream of coconut

If you have a bar cart, the lower shelf is where you would keep your bitters, unopened vermouth, a few mixers, red wine, and your garnishes.

Fresh lemons and limes should also always be on your bar cart as they are essential to so many types of cocktails. Some people prefer to store citrus in the refrigerator, where it will keep longer; however, just make sure to bring it up to room temperature before squeezing, to ensure maximum juice extraction. The other citruses, fruits, and herbs may be used slightly less frequently, but are useful to keep in stock nonetheless.

In the refrigerator, you should also keep your aromatized and forti-fied wines once they've been opened, plus white wine, Champagne, or sparkling wine ready for use. Your homemade cocktail cordials, such as simple syrup, fruit syrups, shrubs, and lemon cordial, should also be stored in the refrigerator. Although not strictly necessary, it's usually a good idea to keep a few mixers, such as club soda, tonic, and ginger beer, chilling as well. Otherwise, you can store them in the pantry with the other dry cocktail goods, including cans or bottles of pineapple juice, cranberry juice, cream of coconut, and tomato juice.

THE TEA CABINET

You may not have been expecting to hear that you'd need to stock a tea cabinet from a guidebook on cocktails! However, if you want to mix all the way through to the end of this book, you will need to keep some teas on hand to make the original spirit-free cocktails in the final chapter. The good news is that the tea cabinet is significantly cheaper to keep well stocked than the bar cart and, if you're anything like me, you will find plenty of other occasions to make use of your teas outside of cocktail hour. The teas used in this book are:

+ White—white Earl Grey
+ Green—green, jasmine green
+ Oolong—oolong
+ Black—lapsang souchong, chai
+ Herbal—mint, chamomile, hibiscus

Ideally, tea should be made using loose leaves in a porcelain or china teapot, either with an internal infuser or strained through a tea strainer.

THE GLASS CABINET

Finally, the glassware. Ten styles of cocktail glass are used throughout this book, including the collins, highball, double old-fashioned, cocktail glass, coupe, flute, tiki mug, wineglass, julep cup, and shooter or shot glass. If you like collecting stuff, you may well have most of these styles in your cabinet already. However, this is *not* a necessity. It's less about having a glass in every style, and more about having one or two glasses that will suit most of the drinks that *you* like to serve on *your* home menu.

For me, the Swiss Army knife of the glassware world is always going to be the stemless wineglass. The stemless wineglass is simply elegant and functionally ideal, and a must for hosting parties. Stemless wineglasses are relatively cheap to buy in bulk, will not tip over easily, and stack neatly in the dishwasher for fast cleanup. There are very few cocktails that could not be served elegantly in a stemless wineglass.

In addition to a few special glasses, you may also want to invest in a punch bowl, pitcher, or decanter for batched drinks, plus some small decorative bowls for garnishes.

Most important, serve your cocktails in vessels that make *you* happy. The meaning of a cocktail is not simply in the liquids coming together, but also in the intention of the host and the manner in which you mark the occasion. A glass that has a story behind it—passed on from a dear family member, discovered at a random flea market, gifted on some special occasion, etc.—will make any drink taste that much lovelier.

I

THE
DOMESTIC
HOSTESS

c. 1800–1860

Let the strangers see that the women of the house
have proper manners. If you think you'll feel better with something in
your hands, make some milk punch, and take it in to them.
—ELIZA LESLIE, 1837

In the early 1800s, a mixed alcoholic beverage made from spirits, bitters, sugar, and water became all the rage in the gentlemen's clubs and hotel bars of North America. This simple drink, known as the "cocktail," would later go on to define a whole genre of beverages and mark a tradition of American hospitality that would spread the world over.

Private men's clubs, which became prevalent through the 19th century, were establishments where upper-class gentlemen could gather to sip on cocktails in a home-away-from-home environment while nurturing business relationships and debating the politics of the day. Later, as saloons emerged across the growing towns and cities of America, men of all social classes had a place to meet with their peers and merrily drink their distractions away. Therefore, for men at least, the mixed spirit beverage that became known as the cocktail was a symbol of leisure, relaxation, and entertainment from the very start.

In contrast, women of any social standing were excluded from these male-only drinking spaces for most of the 19th century. Instead, they were required by custom to do most of their socializing, and drinking, at home. Since women had responsibility for managing both the health and the social life of the family, the preparation of liquor and alcoholic beverages in the home was part of a much wider system of home management. For the Domestic Hostess, therefore, the cocktail, and alcohol more generally, was not simply a symbol of leisure and relaxation, it was one of domestic responsibility.

THE FIRST COCKTAIL BOOK

The first comprehensive guide to the cocktail ever produced is widely considered to be the *Bar-Tender's Guide*, published in 1862 by professional barman Jerry Thomas. Jerry was one of the most prolific bartenders of his age and a celebrity of his trade, and the release of his book set off a chain reaction in the world of mixology that spread across North America and beyond.

The first half of the *Bar-Tender's Guide*, which was penned by Jerry and was titled "How to Mix Drinks, or the Bon Vivant's Companion," was a professional resource for the compounding of drinks using distilled spirits and other ingredients including bitters, liqueurs, fortified wines, and fruit. The second half of the *Bar-Tender's Guide*, called "A Manual for the Manufacture of Cordials, Liquors, Fancy Syrups etc," was contributed by Swiss liquor distiller and manufacturer Christian Schultz. This section contained commercial recipes for cordial liquors and other preparations used as ingredients in cocktails.

A great number of the cordial liquors used in the *Bar-Tender's Guide*, however, were preparations that women had been making in the home for generations, long before they were ever mixed recreationally into bar drinks. These cordials were used to preserve seasonal produce, treat disease, promote health, mix into other drinks, and flavor foods. Domestic Hostesses kept their recipes for cordial liquors in handwritten books known as the family receipt book.

THE FAMILY RECEIPT BOOK

When the colonial settlers first arrived in the New World, one of the most important personal items they brought with them was the family receipt book containing many lifetimes' worth of handwritten recipes and housekeeping wisdom. These books usually belonged to the lady of the house and were typically passed on through the maternal line from mother to daughter at the time of marriage. One of the most famous family receipt books that still survives today belonged to Martha Washington, the first First Lady of the United States of America. Martha's receipt book was said to have arrived with her ancestors from England sometime around 1650, and Martha later passed along the book to her granddaughter Eleanor Parke Custis on the occasion of Eleanor's marriage. The book continued to be passed down through the generations until it was eventually published by culinary historian Karen Hess in 1981.

Of course, the main drawback of the family receipt system was the need for books to be constantly copied as successive generations of the family branched out. As one 19th-century writer, Sarah Rutledge, explained, "The manuscript, in which is gathered a whole lifetime's experience, cannot be in possession of more than one family in ten. It rarely happens that more than one woman in three generations takes the pains to collect and arrange receipts." Therefore, from the early 1600s onward, women also began writing and publishing household guides for commercial sale.

Seventeenth-century British writer Hannah Woolley is believed to be the first woman to make her living as a domestic writer and published numerous books for housekeepers that covered topics ranging from cooking to embroidery to letter-writing. She was also an amateur physician and authored texts on distillation and homemade medicine production using alcohol as the main ingredient. For example, one of her most famous works, the 1670 book *The Queen-Like Closet*, includes a great number of medicinal formulae for cordial liquors as well as an early recipe for the popular British beverage, punch.

Throughout the 18th and 19th centuries, naval records show that British books on household management written by women continued to be shipped in large numbers to North America. For example, one of the most successful around the turn of the 19th century was *The Art of Cookery, Made Plain and Easy*, by Hannah Glasse, which was first published in 1747. Hannah's book showed colonial women how to cook British and European dishes; how to ferment wine, brew beer, distill spirits; as well as how to compound cordial liquors to treat a broad range of ailments in the home, from such diseases as plague to everyday complaints like indigestion.

Books like Hannah's, and others written by women, would have been in wide circulation in the houses of Domestic Hostesses at the time that bartenders like Jerry Thomas were first learning the skill of mixology. It's therefore highly probable that Jerry and his contemporaries would have been exposed to recipes for cordial liquors and other common ingredients in the home long before they found their way into bars for the purposes of cocktails.

THE CORDIAL HOSTESS

Cordial liquors were alcohol-based tonics that were first produced in Europe from around the Middle Ages. Named for the Latin word *cordis*, meaning "of the heart," the original cordials were botanically infused liquors sipped remedially to invigorate the heart, enliven the spirit, and fortify the body. As they were often sweetened with sugar and flavored with fruit to make them more palatable, it was not long before they were being enjoyed recreationally as well. Indeed, it was the keen interest of the French in sipping their *cordial liqueurs* at parties during the 18th century that gave rise to the word we now use for this category of infused spirits today: *liqueurs*.

Cordials were made by infusing or distilling a custom blend of herbs, fruits, nuts, or spices into a base of neutral spirits or brandy. At first, cordial preparations were produced only in apothecaries or distilleries, but by the 18th century, it had become common practice for resourceful homemakers to make their own. Over time, the use of the word *cordial* lost its medical association and evolved in everyday vernacular to refer to any type of fruit concentrate made from any type of base (including alcohol, vinegar, or fruit juice), as well as to the end drink that could be made using one. Today, however, we would most likely refer to a nonalcoholic fruit concentrate as a *syrup*, to its vinegar-based cousin as a *shrub*, to an infused alcoholic spirit as a *liqueur*, and to a mixed drink as a *cocktail*.

In the early 19th century, back when Jerry Thomas was just starting his bartending career, Domestic Hostesses were already using cordials in myriad ways in the home. For example, they would give cordials by the teaspoon to treat such ailments as cough, fever, or upset stomach; mix them into a dessert or cake for extra flavor; sip them neat after dinner to aid in digestion; and top them with water for a refreshing beverage during hot weather.

In fact, it was customary throughout the 19th century for Domestic Hostesses to welcome their female guests into the parlor after dinner with a glass of their homemade cordial while the men took their brandies in the dining room. To this day, therefore, the word *cordial* refers not only to this type of infused spirit, but also to a particular manner of hosting that is especially courteous and heartfelt. It's fair to say, therefore, that the cordial was not simply a cocktail ingredient but a whole hosting philosophy pioneered and championed by women.

THE FIRST DOMESTIC GODDESS OF AMERICA

In the early 1800s, the majority of cooking and housekeeping books circulating in North America had been mostly reprints of English texts. However, this all changed in 1824 with the publication of Mary Randolph's *The Virginia Housewife*.

Mary Randolph was a southern hostess from an influential Virginia family with close ties to President Thomas Jefferson. For many years, she enjoyed the charmed life of a high society hostess, until one day her husband fell out with the president and lost his high-ranking position in the state. With the couple down on their luck, Mary decided to open a boardinghouse in Richmond to help make ends meet. She quickly gained a reputation as one of the best cooks in Virginia, and in 1824 published her recipes in a cookbook called *The Virginia Housewife*. The book was an instant success, reportedly going through more than 19 editions in the years leading up to the Civil War, and to this day, it is widely considered the definitive text on Virginia cuisine and the first truly American cookbook.

Mary contributed many liquor recipes to *The Virginia Housewife* that are still recognizable as essential cocktail ingredients, including cherry- and rose-flavored brandies; raspberry-, peach-, mint-, and lemon-flavored cordials; and a cherry shrub made with brandy that she wrote was "delicious mixed with water" in the summertime.

TO LIVE WELL,
AND TO BE WELL WHILE WE LIVE

Most early American home writers, like Mary, covered the use of alcohol in food recipes, yet many were cautious about discussing spirits in beverages because of the emerging social discourse around temperance. While, during this early phase of the temperance movement, the emphasis was more on moderation in all things than it was on total abstinence, consuming spiritous liquors was nevertheless viewed as detracting from a healthy lifestyle, alongside such other dubious behaviors as staying up past midnight, overeating, and not spending enough time outdoors.

An influential voice in the early temperance movement was Sarah Hale, a well-known author of novels, short stories, and children's books, and editor of the popular magazine *Godey's Lady's Book*. As the arbiter of good taste for one of the nation's most successful women's magazines, Sarah's mission was to teach her readers "how to live well, and to be well while we live." In 1839, she published one of several successful household management books, *The Good Housekeeper*, in which she promoted the temperance principle that fermented ales and wine could be consumed "very sparingly," but that distilled spirits "should never be considered drinkable" except "sometimes, as a medicine."

Sarah's view, as was the view of most early leaders of the temperance movement, was that the overconsumption of liquor would interfere with "the happiness and usefulness of domestic life." However, as we shall come to see later on, even Sarah's hard line on this would become challenged when certain cocktails, such as the Mint Julep, started to become popular among women of high society. Moreover, not all of the writers for *Godey's Lady's Book* held back on their use of alcohol at this time. One of the more open-minded contributors to the magazine was highly popular 19th-century author Eliza Leslie.

LADIES WHO PUNCH

Much like Mary Randolph, Eliza Leslie had learned her trade as a cook and housekeeper by helping to run her widowed mother's boarding-house during the early 1800s. She also attended classes at one of the first cooking schools in America—Mrs. Goodfellow's of Philadelphia—and in 1828, had successfully published a book, *Seventy-Five Receipts for Pastry, Cakes, and Sweetmeats*, with recipes gleaned from the class. In 1832, she followed up with a second book, *Domestic French Cookery*, an English translation of a French cookbook that included other miscellaneous receipts. The success of her first two books paved the way in 1837 for her to publish her masterwork, *Directions for Cookery, in its Various Branches.*

In *Directions for Cookery*, Eliza covered the gamut of necessities that a woman in 1830s America might need to run her household. Unlike Sarah, she was not shy about including distilled spirits in her writing, and indeed had already shared a recipe for punch under "Miscellaneous Receipts" in her earlier French cookbook. She reproduced the same punch recipe (now retitled as Regent's Punch), plus half a dozen more, in *Directions for Cookery*.

Eliza's knowledge of the flowing bowl was also evident throughout the rest of that book; for example, in her recipes for capillaire ("you may sweeten punch with it"), Curaçao ("a great improvement to punch"), homemade arrack ("a little of it will be found to impart a very fine and fragrant flavor to punch"), and lemon brandy (a good use for leftover peels "when you use lemons for punch or lemonade").

Like the family receipt book, the family punch bowl was a treasured heirloom typically passed down through the maternal line. Indeed, Martha Washington famously bequeathed her punch bowl (described in her will as "the bowl that has a ship in it") to her grandson, George Washington Parke Custis, who in turn passed it on to his own daughter, after a lifetime of service at Mount Vernon happy hours and presidential receptions. The punch bowl was usually kept on display at all times in the parlor and cared for by the lady of the house. In Eliza's fictional short stories, which she published contemporaneously with her recipe books, she described the fastidious way in which women prepared punch to serve visitors in their parlors, revealing the important role they played in the custom at the time.

In addition to punch tips, Eliza provided recipes for other spiritous drinks in *Directions for Cookery*: sangaree and negus (a wine cocktail similar to sangria); such liqueurs as ratafia, noyau, and cherry bounce; and many flavors of alcoholic cordial, including rose, lemon, aniseed, clove, cinnamon, strawberry, raspberry, quince, peach, apricot, and plum. She also gave instructions for the production of homemade bitters—an essential ingredient in cocktails—which she recommended as "a good tonic, taken in a small cordial glass about noon."

A WEAKNESS FOR JULEPS

Eliza Leslie's *Directions for Cookery* was one of the most successful American housekeeping books of the 19th century, reportedly selling over 150,000 copies and going through more than 60 editions. With every new edition, Eliza came under pressure to add new recipes and expand the scope of the book, and so in 1847, she upped her game with the release of *The Lady's Receipt-Book*. Unlike *Directions for Cookery*, which was aimed at a middle-class audience, *The Lady's Receipt-Book* was written for a higher class of "families who possess the means and the inclination to keep an excellent table, and to entertain their guests in a handsome and liberal manner."

A notable addition to the drinks menu in *The Lady's Receipt-Book* was a recipe for the now highly fashionable Mint Julep cocktail. Originally deriving from a camphor and brandy compound used medicinally by the British, the Mint Julep was a recreational beverage made from fresh mint, sugar, and brandy that had been popular in the South from around the turn of the century. Earlier southern writers, such as Mary Randolph and Lettice Bryan (author of the 1839 *The Kentucky*

Housewife) had not included the Mint Julep in their cookbooks, but they had provided recipes for brandy-based mint cordials "to preserve the juice to use when the fresh materials cannot be procured," which were likely used as ingredients to make one.

Around the same time as these books were published, a British writer by the name of Captain Frederick Marryat took a trip around the United States and observed the proclivity of upper-class American ladies to enjoy Mint Juleps, noting it in his travel journal, *Diary in America*, which he published in 1839. In the book, he recalls, "I once overheard two ladies talking in the next room to me, and one of them said, 'Well, if I have a weakness for any one thing, it is for a mint julep.'" Captain Marryat himself found the Mint Julep to be "like the American ladies—irresistible," and described the recipe in detail in his book.

Curiously, though Captain Marryat clearly did not invent the Mint Julep, his recipe somehow went on to become the gold standard in a lot of cookbooks during the mid- to late 19th century. Eliza Leslie's recipe in *The Ladies' Receipt-Book* bears a strong resemblance to his, and it also appears almost word for word in an "American receipt" in *Modern Cookery for Private Families*, by British writer Eliza Acton, which was released in the United States in 1845. Eliza Acton's book, which was fully "revised and prepared for American housekeepers" after its first edition to include the drink, was edited by none other than temperance leader and housekeeping influencer Sarah Hale. It seems that Sarah must have put her temperance beliefs temporarily behind her to help out on the book, because just a few years later in 1852 she included the very same Mint Julep recipe in her own *The Ladies' New Book of Cookery*.

It's unknown how many Domestic Hostesses would have had access to Captain Marryat's published diaries in the United States. However, it is widely known that both Eliza Leslie and Eliza Acton's books were huge best sellers and went through multiple editions through the mid- to late 19th century. Furthermore, it is also known that their recipes were widely copied and frequently reappeared in books and articles by other writers of the period. It is therefore easy to surmise that their decision to include the good captain's Mint Julep recipe in their works would have likely played a significant part in how it came to be established in the folklore of the drink.

ALL THE LADIES LOVE A COBBLER

One of the defining features of the Mint Julep was its magnificent presentation—sprigs of fresh mint projecting from a mound of crushed ice domed high over a frosted metal tumbler. The key ingredient of ice had become available in wealthier households in North America sometime around the 1830s, thanks to the commercial harvesting of lakes in the northern states and its transportation via rail to the South. The icebox—a precursor to the refrigerator—was also invented around this time, and indeed Mary Randolph had famously included a sketch of her own icebox in the second edition of *The Virginia Housewife* in 1825. Alongside ice, the other technological advancement pertinent to the cocktail was the invention of the drinking straw. With ice and straws now widely available, the floodgates for icy cocktails flew open, setting the stage for one of the most popular cocktails of the 19th century to make its entrance: the Sherry Cobbler.

The Sherry Cobbler took off in a big way in the United States sometime around the 1830s, especially among women. An early clue to the feminine appeal of the Sherry Cobbler came in 1838, when British diarist and artist Katherine "Janie" Ellice mentioned one in a travelogue of a trip she took to upstate New York with her husband, who was then private secretary to the governor of Canada. Janie described tasting both the Mint Julep and the Sherry Cobbler on her trip but preferred the cobbler, noting that it was both "delicious & easy of composition," and recorded the recipe in her diary for posterity.

By the 1840s, the Sherry Cobbler started appearing on bar menus and home menus across the country. One of the first domestic receipts for the drink can be found in the work of another influential southern hostess from the period, Sarah Rutledge of Charleston, South Carolina, who included it in her celebrated cookbook *The Carolina Housewife*, published in 1847. Sarah noted in the foreword to the book that she did not want to repeat directions that were found in "Miss Leslie's excellent 'Directions for Cookery,' and in many others of similar character," but instead to share recipes from "receipt books of friends and acquaintances," where "it is believed the receipts are original." Perhaps this is why she chose to include the Sherry Cobbler over the Mint Julep, which had already been published in Eliza's *The Ladies' Receipt-Book*. Not to be outdone, of course, Eliza added the Sherry Cobbler recipe to her final cookbook, the 1857 *Miss Leslie's New Cookery Book*.

DOMESTIC CORDIALS

While recipes in early housekeeping books demonstrate that Domestic Hostesses may have created many of the cordials that were later used in cocktails, it is not always clear where their recipes originally came from. Some would have surely come from the authors' family receipt books, while others were likely copied from other books or magazines of the time. However, it is also likely that quite a number would have been appropriated from servants and enslaved workers in the authors' households. Since very few enslaved women in the late 18th and early 19th centuries were taught to read or write, they rarely, if ever, received credit in housekeeping guides. Furthermore, female domestic workers were often banned from coming into contact with liquor entirely, under strict orders to "touch not, taste not, handle not" if they expected to keep their reputations intact.

The first Black female cook to publish a household management guide, which happened also to include alcohol-based cordials, was Malinda Russell, with *A Domestic Cookbook* in 1866. Malinda was a third-generation free woman who had learned her trade as a cook in Virginia from another Black cook by the name of Fanny Steward and had also spent six years running a bakery business in Tennessee. After a series of rather harrowing life events, including being widowed, robbed of her life savings, and caring for her son who had special needs, Malinda self-published *A Domestic Cookbook* in an effort to support herself through her senior years. Modeling the recipes "after the plan of the Virginia Housewife" by Mary Randolph, the book included many unique recipes for baked goods and desserts, as well as for blackberry, strawberry, peach, and quince cordials.

Although home preparation of cordials may have declined in the years since the early Domestic Hostesses, the basic techniques of cordial making, as advanced by the likes of Martha Washington, Mary Randolph, Eliza Leslie, and Malinda Russell remain as essential to cocktails today as they did two centuries ago. The recipes on the pages that follow are adapted from these early household receipts with simple ingredients and straightforward techniques that are easy to execute in kitchens to this day. Keeping a few of these homemade cordials on hand in your cocktail pantry is a sure-fire way to take your hosting game to the next level while paying tribute to the early days of domestic cocktail production.

COCKTAIL CORDIALS

SIMPLE SYRUP

Makes 2 cups of syrup

A simple syrup of sugar and water was used in many 19th-century home recipes and is still a staple ingredient in a great many cocktails today. Adding sugar to a cocktail not only heightens its flavors, but also improves its viscosity.

1 cup cane sugar   **1 cup water**

Combine the sugar and water in a small saucepan and slowly bring the water to a boil. When the mixture starts to boil, turn off the heat and stir to dissolve the sugar. Let the mixture cool, then store in a glass jar. The syrup will keep in the refrigerator for up to 3 weeks.

+ *FLAVOR INSPIRATION:*
   Add a few drops of orange flower water to the syrup to make a version of Eliza Leslie's capillaire. Capillaire can be used in cocktail recipes wherever simple syrup is called for and will add a light floral piquancy to a drink.

CLASSIC VARIATION

HONEY SYRUP
Makes 2 cups of syrup

1 cup honey   1 cup water

Combine the honey and water in a small saucepan and slowly bring to a boil. When the mixture starts to boil, turn off the heat and stir to dissolve the honey. Let the mixture cool, then store in a glass jar. The syrup will keep in the refrigerator for up to 3 weeks.

RASPBERRY SYRUP
Makes approximately 2 cups of syrup

Early Domestic Hostesses, such as Mary Randolph, relied on fruits and herbs that were native to North America, including raspberry, mint, and peach, to make their original cordials, flavors that continued to be popular in drinks throughout the 19th century. Making your own raspberry syrup also makes a great alternative to grenadine in classic cocktail recipes.

1½ cups fresh raspberries   1 cup water
1 cup cane sugar

Combine all the ingredients in a pan and bring the water to a boil. Simmer gently for 5 minutes. Turn off the heat and allow the mixture to cool for a further 30 minutes. Strain the syrup into a glass bottle or jar for storage. The syrup will keep in the refrigerator for up to 3 weeks.

+ *FLAVOR INSPIRATION:*
   Try a combination of berries, such as blackberries, strawberries, cranberries, cherries, or blackcurrants.

CLASSIC VARIATIONS

MINT SYRUP

Makes approximately 2 cups of syrup

1 cup fresh mint leaves   1 cup water
1 cup cane sugar

Combine all the ingredients in a pan and bring the water to a boil. Simmer gently for 1 minute. Turn off the heat and allow the mixture to cool for a further 30 minutes. Strain the syrup into a glass bottle or jar for storage. The syrup will keep in the refrigerator for up to 3 weeks.

PEACH SYRUP

Makes approximately 2 cups of syrup

1½ cups chopped fresh or   1 cup cane sugar
    frozen peaches   1 cup water

Combine all the ingredients in a pan and bring the water to a boil. Simmer gently for 5 minutes. Turn off the heat and allow the mixture to cool for a further 30 minutes. Strain the syrup into a glass bottle or jar for storage. The syrup will keep in the refrigerator for up to 3 weeks.

LEMON CORDIAL

Makes approximately 2 cups of cordial

Sometimes called a sherbet, the lemon cordial made from oleo saccharum (lemon oil infused into sugar) and lemon juice was an essential ingredient in punches and cups and also the base for a delicious "portable lemon-ade" in the 19th century. Make sure to take only the top layer of zest from the fruit and none of the underlying pith when peeling the lemons, to preserve the oil only.

Peel of 8 lemons	Juice of 8 lemons (should
1 cup cane sugar	equal 1 cup)

Place the lemon peels in a glass jar, cover with the sugar, and let stand for 1 to 2 hours, until the oil of the lemon peels is visibly separated and starts to form a syrup on top of the sugar. Add the lemon juice to the jar and shake gently until the sugar is dissolved, which can take up to 30 minutes. Then, strain the sweetened lemon juice through a sieve to remove the peels, reserving the resulting cordial in a glass jar. The cordial will keep in the refrigerator for up to 3 weeks.

+ *FLAVOR INSPIRATION:*
  This cordial can be made with any type of citrus. Try lime, orange, tangerine, grapefruit, or a combination.

CLASSIC DRINKS

LEMONADE
Makes 1 drink

1 ounce Lemon Cordial   4 ounces water

Fill a collins glass with ice. Add the cordial and water and stir gently to mix.

✦ *FOR A PITCHER:*

First combine 1 cup of cordial and 1 quart of water in a large pitcher and stir. Fill the remainder of the pitcher with ice and garnish with lemon slices. Makes 8 servings.

PINK LEMONADE
Makes 1 drink

½ ounce Lemon Cordial   4 ounces water
½ ounce Raspberry Syrup
  (page 37)

Fill a collins glass with ice. Add the lemon cordial, raspberry syrup, and water and stir gently to mix.

✦ *FOR A PITCHER:*

First combine ½ cup of lemon cordial, ½ cup of raspberry syrup, and 1 quart of water in a large pitcher and stir. Fill the remainder of the pitcher with ice and garnish with lemon slices and fresh raspberries. Makes 8 servings.

CHERRY SHRUB

Makes approximately 1½ cups of shrub

Cherries are native to North America. A cherry shrub made with brandy was a popular cordial to mix with water for a refreshing beverage in the summertime. With the advent of temperance in the early 19th century, however, vinegar became a popular replacement for the brandy. The first fruit-and-vinegar-based "shrub" is believed to have been published by Lydia Maria Child in The Frugal Housewife *in 1829.*

2 cups fresh or thawed frozen cherries, pits removed

1 cup cane sugar
½ cup red wine vinegar

Mix the fruit and sugar together in a glass jar, seal, and allow to macerate in the refrigerator for 1 to 2 days. When the fruit is soft, add the vinegar to the jar and shake gently to dissolve the sugar. Strain the shrub through a fine-mesh sieve into a clean jar. Store in the refrigerator and wait a week before using. The shrub will keep in the refrigerator for up to 6 months.

✦ FLAVOR INSPIRATION:
For a zesty twist, try adding ½ cup of chopped ginger to the cherries, or add a few whole spices, such as cinnamon, clove, or star anise.

CLASSIC DRINK

SHRUB COCKTAIL

Makes 1 drink

½ ounce Cherry Shrub
4 ounces club soda

Garnish: lime wedge

Fill a collins glass with ice. Pour in the shrub and club soda and stir gently to mix. Squeeze the lime wedge lightly over the drink before dropping it in.

CURAÇAO

Makes approximately 1 liter of liqueur

Curaçao, an orange and brandy liqueur used in many classic cocktails, is easily made at home. The recipe uses both sweet oranges, such as the widely available navel or Cara Cara varieties, and bitter oranges, such as the Seville. However, if bitter oranges are unavailable, such writers as Eliza Leslie recommended the alternative of "shaddock" (pomelo) or grapefruit. In a classic variation, vodka is used instead of brandy for the lighter style Triple Sec. In both recipes, make sure to peel only the top layer of zest from the fruit and none of the underlying pith, to avoid unwanted bitterness.

Peel of 8 sweet oranges
Peel of 2 bitter oranges or
1 pink grapefruit

One 750 ml bottle
brandy or cognac
1 cup Simple Syrup
(page 36)

Mix the peels and liquor together in a large glass jar and seal. Allow the peels to macerate in a cool, dark place until the liquid smells and tastes strongly of orange (5 to 7 days). Strain the liquor through a coffee filter into a clean jar to remove the peels, then add the simple syrup and stir to combine. This liqueur will keep for up to a year stored in a cool, dark place.

CLASSIC VARIATION

TRIPLE SEC
Makes approximately 1 liter of liqueur

Peel of 8 sweet oranges
Peel of 2 bitter oranges or
  1 pink grapefruit

One 750 ml bottle vodka
1 cup Simple Syrup
  (page 36)

Mix the peels and liquor together in a large glass jar and seal. Allow the peels to macerate in a cool, dark place until the liquid smells and tastes strongly of orange (5 to 7 days). Strain the liquor through a coffee filter into a clean jar to remove the peels, then add the simple syrup and stir to combine. This liqueur will keep for up to a year stored in a cool, dark place.

II

THE
LADY
HOSTESS

c. 1860–1900

Every lady should know how to mix cup, as it is convenient both for
supper and lawn-tennis parties, and is preferable in its effects to the
heavier article so common at parties—punch.
—MARY SHERWOOD, 1884

After the Civil War, the rapid acceleration of wealth in cities like New York, Philadelphia, Boston, and Chicago led to the emergence of a new social class in America. Many families who just a generation ago had been living modest lives in semirural towns were being joined by immigrants flooding in from Europe, all looking to get their shot at financial prosperity in the big city. For the fortunate few who were in the right place at the right time, there was suddenly untold wealth at their disposal.

Consequently, the social order of upper-class America during the late 19th century was in a constant state of flux and the struggle for new money households to be accepted by the dominant names of the old-world order was real. While the male heads of households gained their reputation through their commercial successes, it was down to their wives to build their family's social standing. It was from this dynamic that a new hostess emerged. The Lady Hostess had the responsibility of not only overseeing the management of a grand estate and large household, but leveraging her domestic skills with the sole purpose of gaining higher social status for her family. All she needed to know was the right way to do it.

THE CULT OF DOMESTICITY

During the late 1700s and early 1800s, households in America had mostly operated as self-sufficient units with a family's economy largely tied to generational wealth and the productivity of the household itself. While men and women were often engaged in different tasks around the homestead, they were mostly living and working alongside one another, gathering once a day to share a large meal in the early afternoon. However, by the late 1800s, this pattern of life and work in America changed dramatically as the growing economy, buoyed by rapid industrialization, pushed workers toward the fast-growing cities. During the late 1800s, urban men would leave the house for work early in the morning and not return until late in the evening, leaving women with the sole responsibility of managing the household.

This created not only a clear division between public life and private life, but also between what Victorians deemed to be "male" and "female" behaviors. These gender-based activities were reinforced culturally by prevailing beliefs about the inherent biological nature of men versus women. For example, women were believed to be morally strong yet physically weak, which supposedly made them more suited to the quiet life of the home; while men were deemed to be physically strong yet morally weak, which made them apparently better equipped to handle the brash and risky world of politics and commerce.

And just as men had to prove their worth in their economic roles, women were expected to perform their domestic duties to the highest levels as well. This resulted in the "cult of domesticity" that would dominate the way women conducted their home and social lives for close to half a century.

BEETON'S *BOOK OF HOUSEHOLD MANAGEMENT*

One of the heroes of the domestic movement was British writer Isabella Beeton. Isabella started her writing career in the 1850s penning short stories and cookery columns for her husband's *The Englishwoman's Domestic Magazine*. He quickly promoted her to editor of the magazine and she soon began writing an expansive monthly supplement that covered cooking and homemaking tips and advice. The endeavor was extremely successful, and in 1861, her articles were published collectively as the *Book of Household Management*. Running to more than 1,100 pages and over 900 recipes, the book was an instant success, reportedly selling over 60,000 copies in its first year of publication.

Realizing she was onto something, Isabella began working on a revised edition of the book. However, her efforts were cut short when she tragically passed away not long after giving birth to her fourth child. Grief stricken and cash strapped, her husband was forced to sell the rights to the *Book of Household Management* to another publisher, who continued to distribute the book under Isabella's name. Over the course of the next century, the *Book of Household Management* would go on to become one of the most successful cookbooks of all time, running through seven major editions and, at its peak, reportedly selling hundreds of thousands of copies per year. The book was translated into numerous languages and distributed around the world, turning the posthumous "Mrs. Beeton" into a global household name.

Part of the appeal of Isabella's writing style was not so much in her recipes, many of which were not original, but in the straightforward way in which she shared tips, background notes, and definitions for her readers. For example, in her chapter on beverages, she categorized drinks into three classes: the first was "Beverages of the simplest kind not fermented," including hot drinks like tea and coffee and compounded beverages like lemonade and vinegar-and-water; the second was "Beverages, consisting of water, containing a considerable quantity of carbonic acid," which were fizzy drinks like ginger ale and soda water; and the third was "Beverages composed partly of fermented liquors," or mixed alcoholic drinks, which included traditional beverages like mulled wine, possets and punches, as well as newer style drinks like Claret Cup and the now infamous American Mint Julep.

By clearly delineating what different beverages were and how they were to be used, Isabella's work proved to be not only highly approachable, but also highly influential.

THE CHIEF ENTERTAINER OF THE HOME

The simple style of Isabella's writing meant it had broad appeal with the emerging middle classes in both Britain and North America, and the *Book of Household Management* was widely given as an instructional guide to new wives and newly employed housekeepers during this period. However, the Lady Hostess was constantly looking for bigger and better ways to elevate her social standing and to display her domestic prowess among her peers. One of the most effective ways for her to make the right impression in society was by hosting an intense schedule of formal dinners and receptions where no expense was spared.

In 1877, high society hostess Mary Henderson published one of the most successful dinner guides of the 19th century, a book called *Practical Cooking and Dinner Giving*. Mary was the daughter of a prominent New York judge and wife of a former Missouri senator, and so ideally placed to advise the new school of Lady Hostesses on the intricacies of the formal dinner. This included how to send and respond to invitations, how to correctly set and decorate a dinner table, the right order of service for dinner and other meals, how to greet guests, and what to serve at the table with menus in both English and French.

Hosting etiquette for Lady Hostesses during this time followed very strict codes. For example, when arriving for a dinner, guests were no longer received in the front parlor but shown directly to the drawing room, where they would be greeted by the host and hostess, and from where the men would then escort the women into the dining room. Since the dining room, rather than the parlor, was now the focal point of the drinks and entertainment, it was imperative that it should be decked out impeccably. As one etiquette writer of the period, Mary Sherwood, described, "The people who enter a modern dining-room find a picture before them, which is the result of painstaking thought, taste, and experience, and, like all works of art, worthy of study."

Practical Cooking and Dinner Giving went on to detail how a formal dinner should unfold across 16 courses with the appropriate wines, sherries, and liqueurs to serve throughout the meal. This included the continuing tradition of punch, which would be served at the table by the hostess both at the start of the meal—either with or before the turtle soup—and a second time as a palate refresher usually in between the beef and game courses. This second punch, known as Roman Punch, was not so much a beverage as a boozy sorbet served with a spoon out of a Champagne coupe or sherbet glass.

Roman Punch, or Punch à la Romaine as it was called in the fanciest of houses, had been popular as a dinner course throughout most of the 19th century, with recipes appearing in household management guides from around the 1830s onward. In the beginning, Roman Punch was served much like any other punch—either hot or lightly chilled—but as ice became more widely available, the service of iced or frozen Roman Punch became not only a necessity at a dinner, but the hallmark of the very finest meals. Like other details of the table, the presentation of Roman Punch was often taken to extremes by the Lady Hostess. As Mary Sherwood observed, "When the Roman punch is served it comes in the heart of a red, red rose, or in the bosom of a swan, or the cup of a lily, or the 'right little, tight little' life-saving boat. Faience, china, glass, and ice are all pressed into service of the Roman punch, and sometimes the prettiest dish of all is hewn out of ice."

EVERY LADY SHOULD KNOW HOW TO MIX CUP

Balls, dinners, and evening soirees formed the core of the winter social calendar for the Lady Hostess, but in the summer, the best of society decamped from their brownstones in the city to lush country estates and fancy resorts in places like upstate New York; Long Island; Newport, Rhode Island; and Cape Cod. Here, the cocktail parlor effectively moved outside as social entertainment took the form of extravagant garden parties organized around genteel outdoor pursuits, such as tennis, croquet, and archery. The new sport of lawn tennis had only been introduced around the 1870s in the United States but had taken off quickly among the upper classes, so much so that hosting a few sets at one's country estate became the ultimate mark of social standing.

In 1884, New York City hostess Mary Sherwood, a writer on society life for the likes of *Harper's Bazaar* and the *New York Times*, published a detailed guide to the etiquette of the garden party and similar outdoor gatherings in her best-selling book *Manners and Social Usages*. This included tips on displaying flowers and greenery, designing bounteous menus around seasonal fruits and vegetables, and staging outdoor activities, such as cards, checkers, and croquet. It also included tips on the service of high society's new favorite beverage, the cup.

The cup was a punchlike cocktail, made with wine, soda water, liqueurs, and fruit, and had been popular in Britain from around the mid-1800s; indeed Isabella Beeton had included recipes for both Claret Cup and Champagne Cup in her 1861 *Book of Household Management*. However, the drink took off in a big way in America toward the end of the century. As Mary explained in *Manners and Social Usages*, cups "were not until lately known in America, except at gentleman's clubs and on board yachts, but which are very agreeable mixtures, and gaining in favor." Mary felt that "every lady should know how to mix cup as it is convenient both for supper and lawn-tennis parties, and is preferable in its effects to the heavier article so common at parties—punch."

The low alcohol content and elegant presentation of cups made them widely appealing to women and, alongside the now mainstream popularity of Sherry Cobbler and Mint Julep, they quickly became the beverage of choice, not only for garden parties, but also for ladies' luncheons. In 1892, Mary followed up *Manners and Social Usages* with a second book on etiquette, *The Art of Entertaining*, in which she described the joy of the ladies' lunch. Since women were often frowned upon for drinking more than one glass of wine at a mixed company dinner at this time, a ladies' lunch was an opportunity for hostesses to let loose a little bit. Mary described the ladies' luncheon as "apt to be a lively and exhilarating occasion" and "the best moment in the day for some people."

No doubt this was partly due to the service of cup. As Mary wrote in *The Art of Entertaining*, "Ever since Cleopatra dissolved the pearl, the wine-cup has held the gems of human fancy." Her chapter on lunches provided recipes for such cups as the Champagne Cup and Claret Cup, as well as for other fruity beverages enjoyed by women at the time, including several styles of julep and cobbler, and a drink known as Turkish Sherbet, made with fruit syrup, liquor, and crushed ice.

Like Mary, a number of etiquette and cookbook writers published books promoting the importance of these drinks among women in polite society at around the same period. These included Florence Burton Kingsland's *Etiquette for All Occasions*, Mrs. Charles Moritz and Adele

Kahn's *The Twentieth Century Cookbook*, and Juliet Corson's *Practical American Cookery and Household Management.*

BRINGING THE COCKTAIL HOME

During the Lady Hostess's era, men and women spent much of their days socializing in completely separate spaces—women at their luncheons and teas in other women's houses, and men at their gentlemen's suppers in hotel bars and private clubs. However, toward the end of the 19th century, many hostesses were beginning to question this division and to take a more active interest in what was going on in the public sphere. Their first step toward getting more involved was to try to encourage their husbands to do more of their business at home. One way they thought to achieve this was to re-create some of the comforts, conveniences, and menus of the gentleman's club in the home parlor environment.

In 1893, New York society hostess Dell Montjoy Bradley, who wrote under her husband's name as Mrs. Alexander Orr Bradley, published a short pamphlet titled *Beverages and Sandwiches for Your Husband's Friends, by One Who Knows*, which contained dozens of recipes for punches, cups, and sandwiches—the sort of fare that was likely popular on bar menus at many hotels and clubs of the time. Dell's husband was a well-known financier and member of several New York clubs, and her brother-in-law was general manager of some of the city's top hotels, which no doubt would have given her good insight into the world of the private bar. In her pamphlet, her goal was to show "fin-de-siècle women a solution to that gastronomic problem—the Labyrinthian way to a man's heart" with tips and recipes that would "guarantee entire satisfaction to the most fastidious bon-viveur."

Across the Atlantic, London-based author and columnist Harriet Anne de Salis took a similar approach with her à la Mode series of cookbooks. The first, *Savouries à la Mode*, published in 1886, covered the subject of canapés and appetizers, and was described by one reviewer as satisfying "the fastidious appetites of husbands who are apt to compare the luxuries of a club breakfast with domestic fare." A few years later, in 1891, she followed up with *Drinks à la Mode*, which provided recipes for traditional British punches, cups, and beer drinks, as well as for more contemporary "American Drinks," such as the Whisky Cocktail, Whisky Sour, Bosom Caresser, Eye Opener, and Corpse Reviver.

Drinks à la Mode was published in both London and New York. However, it seems that the British were somewhat nonplussed by the new fashion of fancy drinks emerging from America at this time. One reviewer of the book even went as far as to urge their readers to steer away from such "Transatlantic decoctions with their terrible names" and to stick to the old English "draughts that may be quaffed without danger to health or principles" instead.

THE HOSTESS AND SUFFRAGE

By the turn of the 20th century, women of all social classes in America were growing tired of the rigid social conventions of the Victorian period and of being excluded from participating in matters that were going on outside their own front doors. Despite upper-class women holding immense power in social circles, their influence in business and political circles was effectively nil. As the excesses of the Gilded Age stoked the fires of corruption from the very top to the very bottom of society, young upper-class women began mobilizing behind the suffrage movement and supporting such organizations as the National American Woman Suffrage Association in the fight to remove legal barriers from women voting and tip the balance of power in the country.

At the other end of the class spectrum, huge inequalities in wealth caused by rapid economic advancement during the late 19th century were exacerbating issues of poverty and excess alcohol consumption, especially among working-class men. Working-class women, who due to the Victorian norms of domesticity were often completely economically dependent on men, watched helplessly as their husbands frittered their incomes and reputations away in the rapidly growing male-only saloons of towns and cities across America. By the turn of the 20th century, a new temperance movement had emerged with such groups as the Women's Christian Temperance Union, and the more militant Anti-Saloon League, taking the lead on the campaign for a national prohibition on alcohol.

Over the next two decades, the temperance and suffrage movements would come together to form one of the most powerful political alliances in history that would not only go on to change the law, but male-female drinking culture, forever.

LADY COCKTAILS

Mary Sherwood, Dell Montjoy Bradley, Harriet de Salis, and other etiquette writers of the Lady Hostess era demonstrated how willingly and enthusiastically women of the late 19th century were bringing such drinks as the cobbler, julep, and wine cup into their home for service at dinners, garden parties, and ladies' luncheons. Not only did women embrace these drinks, but they put their own spin on them, too, by adding flavorful fruit cordials and ever more fancy garnishes. A pattern of cocktail embellishment that would be repeated several times over in the next century.

In the recipes that follow, we take the four classes of cocktail most popular during the late 19th century—punch, cup, julep, and cobbler—and present them in their classic form as well as with some of the flavor variations that were popular at the time, using the cocktail cordials we created in the first chapter. As women became more independent drinkers and thinkers over the next two decades, we will see in forthcoming eras how drinks like the wine cup would go on to be reworked and restyled even further with the changing tastes of a new 20th-century hostess—the Tea Party Hostess.

PUNCHES AND COBBLERS

REGENT'S PUNCH

Makes 1 cocktail

This simple punch recipe is adapted from Eliza Leslie's Regent's Punch recipe in her Domestic Cookery, in its Various Branches *in 1837. While the original receipt calls for "any liquor suitable for punch," including brandy, whiskey, rum, or Champagne, my personal preference is for bourbon. The delicious peach variation, Carolina Punch, derives from her final work, the 1857* Miss Leslie's New Cookery Book.

2 ounces bourbon
½ ounce Lemon Cordial
(page 39)

2 ounces brewed green
tea, cooled
Garnish: lemon slice

Combine the bourbon, lemon cordial, and green tea in a rocks glass with a large cube of ice, stir lightly, and garnish with the lemon slice.

+ *FOR A BOWL*

Measure out the same proportions in cups (to serve a group of 4), pints (to serve 8), or quarts (to serve 16), serving over a large block of ice. For optimal results, let the drink sit for an hour or two in the refrigerator before adding the ice. This recipe can also be frozen into a slushy sorbet for service as Roman Punch.

CLASSIC VARIATION

CAROLINA PUNCH
Makes 1 cocktail

2 ounces bourbon
½ ounce Peach Syrup
(page 38)
¼ ounce fresh lemon juice

2 ounces brewed oolong
tea, cooled
Garnish: peach slice

Combine the bourbon, peach syrup, lemon juice, and oolong tea in a rocks glass with a large cube of ice, stir lightly, and garnish with the peach slice.

✦ *FOR A BOWL*

Measure out the same proportions in cups (to serve a group of 4), pints (to serve 8), or quarts (to serve 16), serving over a large block of ice. For optimal results, let the drink sit for an hour or two in the refrigerator before adding the ice.

CHAMPAGNE CUP

Makes 1 cocktail

These Champagne Cup and Champagne Punch recipes are a mash-up between Isabella Beeton's Champagne Cup in her 1861 Book of Household Management, *and Jerry Thomas's Champagne Punch in his 1862* Bar-Tender's Guide.

¼ ounce Curaçao (page 42)
¼ ounce Raspberry Syrup
  (page 37)
¼ ounce Lemon Cordial
  (page 39)

4 to 5 ounces
  Champagne, chilled
Garnishes: fresh raspberry,
  lemon twist

Pour the Curaçao, raspberry syrup, and lemon cordial into a Champagne flute and top with the chilled Champagne. Garnish with the raspberry and lemon twist.

CLASSIC VARIATION

CHAMPAGNE PUNCH

Makes 12 to 15 servings

3 ounces Curaçao (page 42)
3 ounces Raspberry Syrup
  (page 37)
3 ounces Lemon Cordial
  (page 39)

Two 750 ml bottles
  Champagne, chilled
Garnishes: fresh
  raspberries, lemon
  wheels, orange wheels

Combine the Curaçao, raspberry syrup, and lemon cordial in a punch bowl and chill for an hour. When ready to serve, add ice to the bowl and top with the chilled Champagne. Garnish with raspberries and lemon and orange wheels.

MINT JULEP

Makes 1 cocktail

After Captain Marryat's Mint Julep recipe was heavily featured in the home management guides of the Domestic Hostess, it became a mainstay of every late-century etiquette guide. The proper way to mix a Mint Julep is a matter of great regional pride in America, but in truth, the base recipe has changed very little. Bourbon is typically used over brandy today, while the use of a preprepared mint syrup can help save on muddling when mixing for numbers.

2 large mint sprigs, each with 5 or 6 leaves
½ ounce Simple Syrup (page 36) or Mint Syrup (page 38)

2 ounces bourbon

Strip all but three or four of the mint leaves from the sprigs and reserve the remaining sprigs. Muddle the stripped mint leaves with the mint or simple syrup in the bottom of a tumbler or julep cup. Add the bourbon and fill the cup with crushed ice. Stir until the cup starts to frost. Add more ice to create a dome at the top of the glass and garnish with the reserved mint sprigs. Serve with a small straw.

CLASSIC VARIATION

GEORGIA JULEP

Makes 1 cocktail

1 large mint sprig, with 5
or 6 leaves

½ ounce Peach Syrup
(page 38)
2 ounces bourbon

Strip half of the mint leaves from the sprig and reserve the remaining sprig. Muddle the stripped mint leaves with the peach syrup in the bottom of a tumbler or julep cup. Add the bourbon and fill the cup with crushed ice. Stir until the cup starts to frost. Add more ice to create a dome at the top of the glass and garnish with the reserved mint sprig. Serve with a small straw.

SHERRY COBBLER

Makes 1 cocktail

The ideal sherry to use in a cobbler is a medium style, such as amontillado or oloroso. However, cobblers can also be made with red or white port, late harvest and ice wines, or vermouth. As per the garden-party goddess, Mary Sherwood, for the full effect, garnish lavishly with seasonal berries, a maraschino cherry, mint leaves, citrus slices, or a pineapple spear.

2 large orange wheels,
    quartered to make a total
    of 8 pieces
½ ounce Simple Syrup
    (page 36)

3 ounces medium sherry
Garnishes: reserved orange
    wheel pieces, fresh mint,
    fresh berries

Muddle six of the eight orange wheel pieces with the simple syrup in a cocktail shaker, reserving the rest. Add the sherry and ice to the shaker and shake to chill. Strain into a tumbler or julep cup filled with crushed ice and garnish with the remaining orange pieces, mint, and fresh berries. Serve with a small straw.

CLASSIC VARIATION

SHERRY BLUSH

Makes 1 cocktail

3 ounces medium sherry
½ ounce Raspberry Syrup
    (page 37)

Garnishes: fresh
    raspberries, mint

Combine the sherry, raspberry syrup, and ice in a shaker and shake to chill. Strain into a tumbler or julep cup filled with crushed ice and garnish with raspberries and mint. Serve with a small straw.

III

THE
TEA PARTY
HOSTESS

c. 1900–1920

A painter who lacks skill in mixing his colors spoils many a good canvas. So it is with the concocter of drinks. Be his materials never so numerous and pure, if he lacks skill as a compounder; for he will not only mar good ingredients, but disappoint a company.
—AMY LYMAN PHILLIPS, 1906

At the turn of the 20th century, the Gilded Age paved the way for a new middle class to emerge, and with it a New Woman. In the early 1900s, the suffrage movement was picking up steam with women's political ambitions buoyed by their newfound sense of expertise in the domestic realm and by their increasing presence in the workforce outside the home. As women became more engaged in different aspects of public life, they also began to question their right to participate in public social traditions —such as the tradition of men going out to work and having a drink afterward. If men could work, drink, and socialize, why couldn't women?

So, while Carry Nation and her Anti-Saloon League sisters may have been beating down the doors of American saloons to try to shut them down, progressive hostesses of the era were starting a quieter kind of revolution from their parlors. And it all began with that quaintest of feminine rituals—the tea party.

A REVOLUTION IN A TEAPOT

It's hard to imagine the genteel tea party as a symbol of rebellion, yet drinking tea has been a subversive act on the part of women from the very beginning. The first tea gatherings in England were a ladies' social tradition that dated back to the early 1700s, when women, who were excluded from male-occupied coffee shops, began meeting in tea gardens to drink tea instead. At first, only the wealthiest ladies could afford the exotic Chinese leaves, so the women-only tea ceremony emerged as the ultimate symbol of wealth and prestige. However, within a few decades, mass imports of tea made the beverage available to women of every social class, and soon tea and sandwiches were being served in bakeries, tea shops, and home parlors across the United Kingdom.

Tea shops were also some of the first businesses that could be legally owned and operated by British women in the late 1800s and became important hubs for the early suffragette movement. And so, whether served in an elegant tea garden, by the fire in a cozy parlor, or in the back room of a tea shop, the tea party became the hallmark, not only of feminine refinement and sophistication, but also of women's growing sense of independence and political activism.

THE NEW AMERICAN TEA PARTY

Meanwhile, across the pond, etiquette guides throughout the 1800s and early 1900s reveal that the social ritual of the tea party had become just as steeped into the traditions of upper-class American hostesses as it was into those of their British cousins. And just as was happening in Great Britain, at the turn of the 20th century a new type of tea party had begun to emerge in America, too, hosted by a new type of hostess. Not so much the conservative uptown lady but, as the writer Christine Herrick described in 1904, the downtown "college girl, the bachelor maid, the artist, and the so-called Bohemian circle." The Tea Party Hostess began favoring the late afternoon tea party over more formal gatherings for get-togethers like a game of bridge, a birthday celebration, or a pretheater party.

There were several reasons for this trend. Tea parties were much cheaper to organize than a lunch or dinner, so less food was required, much less a team of maids to serve it. The rules of etiquette were also looser. Unlike the expensive wardrobes required for dinner parties, a tea party had no strict dress code. It didn't necessitate a formal invitation, and indeed, it was not uncommon for people to work their way across town, attending multiple sittings in one afternoon. The venue for a tea party was also less fussy. In middle-class houses that lacked the luxury of multiple rooms for entertaining, hostesses began to embrace the idea of keeping one main living area that was elegant enough for guests to be received in style, yet comfortable enough that the family could enjoy it, too. This new-style living room became the ideal venue for the tea party.

The etiquette of the tea party was simple. Hostesses would lay out sandwiches, cakes, and other "dainties" on a side table or serving cart for guests to help themselves. Together with light bites, of course hot beverages, such as tea and coffee, would be served, and so would the centerpiece of the occasion—the wine cup. Inheriting the tradition of the wine cup from the Lady Hostesses, the Tea Party Hostess continued to favor the beverage for its easy composition, low alcohol content, and ornamental appeal. Indeed, the presentation of the cup became a matter of great pride for the Tea Party Hostess, as it was often elaborately garnished for maximum effect with various fruits, herbs, and delicately draped botanical tendrils. As one writer of the period, Helena Judson, emphasized, "There is no end of artistic ways of decorating the glass pitcher or bowl in which a 'fruit cup' or punch is served."

Many of the cocktail and wine cup recipes from the early 20th century are consequently to be found in sandwich books and tea party guides written by women for the purposes of hosting these light tea and cocktail events. These include such titles as *"Dame Curtsey's" Book of Salads, Sandwiches and Beverages*, by Ellye Howell Glover; *Light Entertaining: A Book of Dainty Recipes for Special Occasions*, by Helena Judson; and *Dainties for Home Parties: A Cook-Book for Dance Suppers, Bridge Parties, Receptions, Luncheons and Other Entertainments*, by Florence Williams.

The introduction of booze to the tea party is important most notably because it attracted a new audience who had hitherto shunned the feminine sensibility of the occasion—men. Women began inviting members of the opposite sex to liven up their teatime socializing because it was seen to be a safely chaperoned environment and, with the offer of drinks, the men happily obliged. With men and cocktails came a more spirited atmosphere, and after a few drinks, some dancing might inevitably break out. So, it was not long before these tea *parties* evolved into larger receptions known as tea *dances*. At tea dances, often held in hotels and large reception halls, single men and women would pair up and, after a few rounds of cocktails and wine cup, dance the afternoon away.

Recipes from the era reflect the liveliness of the mood. In her 1915 book *Dainties for Home Parties: A Cook-Book for Dance Suppers, Bridge Parties, Receptions, Luncheons and Other Entertainments*, Brooklyn-based home economics educator Florence Williams shared a great number of recipes designed for such gatherings, with fun names like High Jinks, Ball-Room, L'Amour, Whirligig, and Watch Your Step! Most of these drinks are recognizable as evolutions of earlier cup styles, such as the Claret Cup and Champagne Cup, now updated and rebranded for this more progressive era.

Interestingly, as an aside, the association of the tea party with high jinks would continue on through the 1920s, when teapots would become one of the principal vessels by which cocktails would be covertly served in cafés during the restrictive Prohibition years, and when an invitation to a "tea party" in a hostess's apartment was usually code for cocktails being on the menu. Similarly, the hostess's tea cart, which was basically a two-tiered side table on wheels, would latterly evolve into an important piece of parlor furniture that we now know and recognize to be the bar cart.

OUT OF THE PARLOR, AND INTO THE DANCE HALL

As Tea Party Hostesses were stepping up their hosting game, they began searching for more freedom outside of their domestic roles. The gateway to independence was education and employment. In 1860, only about 1 in 10 women were said to be in paid employment in the United States, but by 1910, it was closer to a quarter. And no longer just in domestic service or manufacturing jobs, either; increasingly, women were getting jobs in clerical and office-based roles, too. Secretarial schools, such as Katharine Gibbs College, popped up in cities around the country, selling women, especially white middle-class women, the dream of financial independence. On the curriculum were such clerical skills as typing and shorthand, but also etiquette and hosting skills—including, of course, the tea party. This New Woman was further epitomized in popular culture by the image of the Gibson Girl—pretty, sporty, artistic, self-assured, and even, dare we say it, temporarily single.

As women started to engage more in certain aspects of economic life, it followed that they began participating more readily in public life, too, infiltrating social spaces—particularly drinking spaces—that had been traditionally reserved for men. For example, women started to eat out more frequently in restaurants, attend public tea dances, as mentioned, and go out to evening cabarets where cocktails were being served. They also frequented ladies-only sections of bars where, in a gender role reversal, men could enter only if accompanied by a woman. And saloons, once the bastion of male-on-male socializing, now opened up their back bar dance halls in an effort to attract a mixed crowd. In 1907, the first private women's club, the Colony Club, opened in New York City, designed by hostess, cocktail lover, and pioneer of interior design Elsie de Wolfe. Wherever cocktails were found, so, increasingly, were women.

MIXOLOGY COMES TO WOMEN

Women's growing interest in cocktails is evident from their writing during this period. In addition to their books on teas and sandwiches, they also began publishing more specialized mixology guides with recipes for spirits-based cocktails that had previously been found only in men's bartending manuals. One of the first comprehensive drinks guides to be written by-women-for-women was Marion Harland and Christine Herrick's *Consolidated Library of Household Cooking and Modern Recipes*, published in 1904. The library was composed of five volumes for the Modern Hostess, the fifth of which was dedicated mostly to drinks.

Marion Harland and Christine Terhune Herrick were a mother-daughter duo who, between them, penned close to 100 books on house-keeping, childcare, cooking, and hosting at the turn of the century. In 1904, they got together to write the *Consolidated Library* with every-thing they felt the modern hostess would need to run and entertain her household. This included a complete education on mixing drinks, selecting wines, and delivering speeches and toasts, with instructions for such classic cocktails as the Manhattan, Martinez, Rickey, Sour, Daisy, and Fizz.

In the introduction to the book, Christine also acknowledged the novelty of her work, quipping that the inclusion of cocktail recipes might finally encourage the men of the house to take more interest in home entertaining. As she wrote, "The fifth volume introduces as innovation in cook-books by being prepared with an especial view to the tastes of the man of the house. Do you think, dear madam, that he has no interest in cook-books? He will be interested in this one! . . . Observe the directions for serving wines, liqueurs, etc. Your lord and master may think himself a judge in this line, but he will be interested in the new features presented here."

Contemporary with the *Consolidated Library* were other books on cocktails, such as May E. Southworth's *One Hundred and One Beverages*, also published in 1904. May's book broke drinks down into the categories of Iced, Summer, Mixed, Hot, Sherbets, Punches, Cordials, and Fruit, and included such eclectic recipes as the Barbed Wire, made with bourbon and sweet apple cider; and the Pacific Union, made from Curaçao, bitters, sweet vermouth, and rye.

In 1906, the fully revised and expanded edition of what was then retitled *Mrs. Beeton's Book of Household Management* included a large section on "American Drinks" categorized, in typical Beeton style, into two distinct groups—the first being "cocktails, or alcoholic fancy beverages" which were described as being "chiefly remarkable for the many ingredients which enter into their composition, the use of various fresh fruits in addition to lemons and oranges, and the extraordinary names bestowed on many of these beverages," and the second being "soda drinks, flavored with fruit syrups or semi-medicinal decoctions."

And in 1909, *The Woman's Dictionary and Encyclopedia: Everything a Woman Wants to Know*, edited by culinary leader Fannie Farmer, recorded its own definition of the cocktail as "a strong stimulating cold American drink composed of spirits, bitters, a little sugar and various aromatic and stimulating assitions [sic]."

THE RISE OF WOMEN CATERERS

It's clear from these books, and others, that women were starting to know their way around cocktails, and it was also around this time that their expertise in the domestic realm was finally beginning to be taken seriously as a discipline outside the home. One of the pioneers of the home economics movement in the United States was Fannie Farmer, who was a principal of the Boston Cooking School and later founder of her own cooking school, as well as an accomplished writer of books on nutrition and culinary science and regular lecturer at such prestigious institutions as Harvard Medical School. By turning the field of domestic work into a science and demonstrating its wider economic value, she and others like her paved the way for women to begin having careers as cooks, caterers, and domestic professionals around the turn of the century.

One such woman who came up with the movement was Black author, entrepreneur, and cooking writer Bertha Turner. While still in her teens, Bertha had started her working life as a servant in the house of an ice manufacturer in Indiana, and then sometime around the turn of the century had taken the bold entrepreneurial step of moving to Southern California to start her own catering business. Bertha's company catered the likes of the famous Club No. 2, the Shakespeare Club, and the prestigious Tea Garden at the Hollywood Bowl in Los Angeles, and she would later go on to become one of the most prominent female business leaders in the city as well as superintendent of domestic science for the State of California.

As catering professionals, Tea Party Hostesses like Bertha were no longer just influencing home menus, but designing commercial menus for some of the most important events and venues of the era, and they were writing up their experiences in books. For example, in 1910, Bertha collaborated with the National Federation of Colored Women to publish *The Federation Cookbook: A Collection of Tested Recipes Contributed by the Colored Women of the State of California*, to which she personally contributed her punch recipes.

BRINGING MEN INTO THE MIX

At the same time as hostesses were professionalizing, they began schooling men on the subject of drinks as well. In 1906, society columnist and hospitality journalist Amy Lyman Phillips published *A Bachelors Cupboard: Containing Crumbs from the Cupboard of the Great Unwedded*, a book specifically aimed at educating the hapless single male on the ways of domestic life. It contained detailed advice on how to furnish and manage an apartment, how to cook and clean, how to entertain and, most important, how to mix drinks.

Comparing mixing drinks to the skill of a painter mixing colors on a canvas, Amy drew on her extensive knowledge of cocktails and interviews with bartenders to produce over 40 recipes for the book. She included many classics in her list as well as new cocktails, such as the Perfect Cocktail, made with equal parts Italian vermouth, French vermouth, gin, and an orange twist, which she described as being all the rage in New York City restaurants at the time. Bearing in mind that Amy herself was barely 30 (and single) when she wrote the book, this was a pretty radical endeavor. Indeed, it would be another 30 years before writing about life for a single *woman* would become even a remotely acceptable prospect. Yet this wouldn't be the last time Amy would break down barriers. Just four years after she published *A Bachelors Cupboard*, she and her sister Gertrude would act as the journalists accompanying Blanche Stuart Scott when she famously became only the second woman in history to drive an automobile solo across the United States, and the first to drive from east to west.

By now, the new independent spirit of women was reverberating on a national level, influencing popular drinks and newly crafted beverages of the era. In 1909, one St. Louis bartender even created a cocktail to commemorate women's progress. Dubbed the Suffragette Cocktail, it was made with equal parts sloe gin, French vermouth, Italian vermouth, a dash of orange bitters, and a lemon twist. The drink was reported in the newspapers to be potent enough that "one makes a man willing to listen to the suffragette's proposition; two convince him that it has some merit; three make him a missionary, willing to spread the gospel abroad; and four make him go home and wash the dishes." One can only imagine what might have been accomplished with more than four of these drinks.

THE COCKTAIL PARTY IS BORN

In addition to tea parties and dances, etiquette books from the turn of the century also reveal that women were now starting to serve cocktails customarily in their homes in the hour before dinner. For example, Fannie Farmer's 1909 *Woman's Dictionary and Encyclopedia* included an entry on "Dinner Cocktails" with drinks recommended to serve before dinner, such as the Manhattan, Martini, or Whisky Sour. And in 1915, Lucy Allen, a former student of Fannie and cofounder of the Boston School of Cookery, described the ritual of serving cocktails and caviar sandwiches as a prelude to dinner in her influential instructional manual *Table Service*. Discussing the order of service, she wrote, "Dinner is announced in the drawing-room by serving the cocktails and sandwiches, the sandwiches being arranged on a doily covered plate . . . one maid passes the cocktails and another follows with the sandwiches."

This predinner drink ritual would very soon become an event in its own right. With women now writing about cocktails, serving drinks in their parlors before dinner, and enjoying alcoholic beverages in restaurants and bars, it was not long before they would invent a new type of party dedicated entirely to the pastime. The first cocktail party was reportedly held on April 15, 1917, by high society hostess Clara Bell Walsh at her father-in-law's home in St. Louis, Missouri. It was described as a midafternoon affair for around 50 guests that took place after church on a Sunday, with a bartender serving up such drinks as the Bronx, Clover Leaf, Sazerac, Martini, and Manhattan.

The media report of the event revealed some curious behaviors at the party; for example, men and women participating equally in the drinking and taking their cocktails standing up. Today, we might take this way of socializing at a cocktail party for granted, but back then, it would have been considered quite avant-garde. What makes Clara's event all the more revolutionary was the fact that, in 1917, about two-thirds of the country was already under some form of Prohibition. Less than three years later, the passing of the 18th Amendment would ban the manufacture, transport, and sale of alcoholic beverages altogether. Clara would go on to become one of the most famous cocktail party hosts of the 20th century—and the American cocktail party tradition, one of its most popular and enduring cultural legacies.

TEA PARTY COCKTAILS

At the turn of the 20th century, Tea Party Hostesses had begun actively participating in cocktail culture and integrating drinks into their own social customs. As well as starting to meet men and cocktails where they were, women had become empowered through such drinks as the wine cup to invent their own drinking rituals and invite men to join in with them, too.

Despite its popularity during this era, however, for some reason the wine cup has often been overlooked in the conventional narrative on the history of the cocktail. Perhaps this was because it was significantly lower in alcohol than other cocktails and so was not considered a "proper" cocktail, or perhaps simply because it was a drink that was primarily favored by women. Nevertheless, looking back, it's evident that the service of wine cup and other cocktails at a tea party and before dinner were precursors to the drinking tradition that would later become known as the cocktail party.

Today, like its Spanish cousin sangria, the wine cup still makes an ideal beverage for early afternoon and outdoor entertaining. It's relatively easy to make, doesn't mind hanging around, and its low alcohol content (around 5 to 7 percent alcohol per volume) means it's highly sessionable. Wine cups usually came in three main styles at the turn of the century, with the most popular being variations on the Claret Cup (a red wine cup), Moselle Cup (a white wine cup), and Champagne Cup (a sparkling wine cup). What set the Tea Party Hostess's wine cups apart from earlier cups, however, was their emphasis on amped up flavor and presentation. Lemons and oranges were the traditional wine cup flavorings, and cucumber plus one or more of the five "cordial flowers" (mint, borage, verbena, marjoram, and pimpernel) would give it botanical depth and interest. The Tea Party Hostess liked to take this a step further by adding more flavor with fruits (e.g., strawberries, raspberries, maraschino cherries, and pineapple), fruit liqueurs (e.g., Curaçao and maraschino), and herbal liqueurs (e.g., Chartreuse and Benedictine).

Writers from this period were also very specific about how wine cups should be prepared. Like punch, wine cups benefit from being mixed well in advance to allow the flavors to mingle, with sparkling water being added just before serving. The purpose of the water is to lengthen the drink, up its refreshment, and reduce its potency. To avoid overdilution, the cup is refrigerated while steeping and then served "on ice" (i.e., the punch bowl rested in a larger bowl of ice), or with a large block of ice to keep it chilled.

One final note on the wine. While there is surely no need to dust off a prized vintage from the cellar to mix up a wine cup, the general rule of thumb is to use no lesser quality than you would otherwise consider drinking as a stand-alone wine. This is to ensure maximum flavor as well as minimum aftereffects the next day.

WINE CUPS

CLARET CUP

Makes 12 to 15 servings

Claret *is the nickname that the British historically gave to red wines from the Bordeaux region of France, and any similar-style red, such as merlot, Malbec, zinfandel, and cabernet sauvignon, works well for this recipe. The Ball-Room version from Florence Williams's 1915 book* Dainties for Home Parties *is a fruitier take on the classic, made with fresh oranges, pineapple, and strawberries.*

One 750 ml bottle medium-
    bodied red wine
4 ounces Curaçao (page 42)
1½ ounces Lemon Cordial
    (page 39)
Peel of ½ cucumber

500 ml sparkling
    water, chilled
Garnishes: lemon wheels
    and cucumber slices,
    fresh lemon balm or
    lemon verbena, or
    fresh mint

Combine the wine, Curaçao, lemon cordial, and cucumber peel in a pitcher and refrigerate for up to 2 hours. Strain into a punch bowl or pitcher and top with the chilled sparkling water. Garnish with lemon wheels, cucumber slices, lemon balm, or mint.

CLASSIC VARIATION

BALL-ROOM
Makes 12 to 15 servings

One 750 ml bottle medium-
    bodied red wine
4 ounces sherry or brandy
1½ ounces Lemon Cordial
    (page 39)
2 strips cucumber peel
3 whole cloves
1 orange, sliced

6 slices pineapple
½ cup sliced strawberries
6 mint sprigs,
    crushed lightly
500 ml sparkling
    water, chilled
Garnishes: fresh mint,
    fresh strawberries

Combine the wine, sherry, lemon cordial, cucumber peel, cloves, orange slices, pineapple slices, strawberry slices, and crushed mint sprigs in a pitcher and refrigerate for up to 2 hours. Strain into a punch bowl or pitcher and top with the chilled sparkling water. Garnish with additional mint and strawberries.

MOSELLE CUP

Makes 12 to 15 servings

Moselle wines, from the Rhine region of Germany, were the base for the popular white cup known as the Moselle Cup in the early 20th century. A medium, fruit-forward white wine, such as Riesling, Gewürztraminer, Chenin Blanc, or Moscato, is ideal, whereas a dessert wine such as sauterne can be used for a sweeter style Sauterne Cup. Florence Williams's Whirligig, from her 1915 book Dainties for Home Parties, *is a slightly more potent version made with rum, the herbal liqueur Chartreuse, pineapple, and maraschino cherries.*

One 750 ml bottle
  white wine
4 ounces Curaçao (page 42)
1½ ounces Lemon Cordial
  (page 39)
Peel and juice of 1 orange

500 ml sparkling water,
  chilled
Garnishes: orange and
  lime wheels, sliced fresh
  strawberries, fresh mint

Combine the wine, Curaçao, lemon cordial, and orange peel and juice in a pitcher and refrigerate for up to 2 hours. Strain and top with the chilled sparkling water in a pitcher or punch bowl. Garnish with orange and lime wheels, sliced strawberries, and mint.

CLASSIC VARIATION

WHIRLIGIG
Makes 12 to 15 servings

375 ml white wine
½ cup rum
½ cup Chartreuse
Juice of 3 lemons
1 cup crushed pineapple
2 oranges, sliced

½ cup maraschino cherries
1 liter sparkling water,
   chilled
Garnishes: pineapple
   rings, orange slices,
   maraschino cherries

Combine the wine, rum, Chartreuse, lemon juice, pineapple, orange slices, and maraschino cherries (reserving those indicated as garnishes) in a pitcher and refrigerate for up to 2 hours. Strain into a punch bowl or pitcher and top with the chilled sparkling water. Garnish with pineapple rings, more orange slices, and a handful of maraschino cherries.

PEACH SHERBET

Makes 20 to 25 small servings

Like its Roman Punch cousin, a sherbet was a slushy frozen fruit dessert served in wide, flat-bottomed coupes as a palate refresher in between food courses at turn-of-the-century dinners. Long before the days of frosé (frozen rosé), it was also popular at many a summertime tea party. This recipe works equally well with white wine, rosé, dessert wine, or Champagne.

2 cups Peach Syrup
(page 38)
Juice of 1 lemon

Juice of 1 orange
One 750 ml bottle white
wine or Champagne

Mix all the ingredients together in a medium bowl, then transfer to a medium freezer-safe container or ice cube trays and freeze for several hours. The mixture will be slushy. Serve in scoops in Champagne coupes or sherbet glasses.

+ *FLAVOR INSPIRATION:*
   This recipe is delicious with any syrup made from stone fruit, such as apricots or light plums. A claret wine version can also be made with darker fleshed fruits, such as cherries or dark plums, and touched up with such spices as cinnamon, star anise, cardamom—or vanilla bean.

BISHOP

Makes 6 to 7 servings

A Bishop was a type of mulled wine that was popular both before and during the Tea Party Hostess's era. Following similar principles to a wine cup, wine is steeped with fruit before being fortified with Curaçao, brandy, or port. Traditionally, the fruit is roasted first, which, if you have time to do it, adds an immensely rich flavor to the drink. May Southworth recommended using zinfandel in her 1904 book One Hundred and One Beverages, *but any fruit-forward red, such as Malbec or Merlot, also works.*

2 whole apples, cored
   and seeded
2 whole tangerines
   or oranges
10 whole cloves
One 750 ml bottle red wine

1½ cups apple cider
2 cinnamon sticks
2 cardamom pods
4 ounces Curaçao
   (page 42)
Garnish: apple slices

If you're roasting your fruits, begin by preheating your oven to 300°F and filling a roasting pan to about a ½-inch depth with freshly boiled water. Stud the apples and tangerines with the cloves and add them to the prepared roasting pan. Roast slowly in the oven for about 2 hours, checking that they do not dry out.

Transfer the cooked apples and oranges to a heavy-bottomed saucepan along with the red wine, apple cider, cinnamon sticks, and cardamom pods. Slowly bring the liquid to a boil on the stovetop and then lower the heat to a simmer. Simmer gently for 15 minutes. Strain the liquid through a fine-mesh sieve to remove the spices and fruits, reserve the liquid, and then stir in the Curaçao. Serve the mulled wine warm in toddy mugs, garnished with a fresh apple slice.

+ *FLAVOR INSPIRATION:*

Mulled wine made with Champagne was known traditionally as a Cardinal, whereas an Archbishop was made with claret; and a Pope, with burgundy. Try it with a few different wine styles and name it after the denominational figurehead of your choosing.

IV

THE
APARTMENT
HOSTESS

c. 1920–1940

Why should men be the only ones to know their
drinks? . . . With seven bottles and a small amount of
knowledge, anyone can be a good hostess
—MARJORIE HILLIS, 1936

On May 21, 1919, the United States House of Representatives approved the Susan B. Anthony Amendment, guaranteeing women the right to vote after more than 70 years of the suffrage campaign led by women. One year later, on August 26, it was officially a part of the United States Constitution, and later, the date would be memorialized forever as Women's Equality Day. And just as 1920 was a big year for women's rights, so it was for cocktails. The 18th Amendment—the prohibition of the manufacturing, transportation, and sale of alcohol within the United States—also went into effect that year after a century-long campaign for temperance, also led in large part by women.

Prohibition banned the sale, manufacture, and transportation of alcohol, but it did not make it illegal to drink. Indeed, it's been widely held that Prohibition was ineffective at curbing people's cocktail drinking habits. From a political point of view, the 18th Amendment was a failure. However, from the point of view of women and the cocktail it was an unmitigated success because it enabled the invention and spread of a new drinking tradition by a new type of hostess in America—the Apartment Hostess.

THE ARRIVAL OF THE COCKTAIL PARTY

During the Tea Party Hostess period, women had already begun hosting mixed company drinks events and venturing out of their tea parlors and into restaurants and dining clubs. However, when bars and drinking clubs closed, drinking was driven underground: first, to speakeasies and illegal dining clubs, and later to the home bar. As a result, women began participating in nightlife in a way they never had before and, as newly empowered and emancipated hostesses, became involved in greater numbers not only in the consuming of cocktails, but in the creation and mixing of them, too.

Now that men and women were socializing and drinking together, in effect women became the key promoters of the cocktail, buoyed by their long-standing role as the chief entertainers of the home. The phenomenon of the cocktail party kicked off in the apartments of well-to-do hostesses across the major cities of the United States in the early 1920s, and over the course of the next two decades, spread like hedonistic wildfire into the suburbs and beyond. Describing the Apartment Hostess in 1923, one journalist even commented, "There are not many ladies in well-to-do houses now—certainly in the Eastern States—who are not experts at making cocktails."

One of the pioneers and early adopters of the phenomenon was Virginia Elliott, a journalist who was in her mid-20s, newly married, and living in midtown Manhattan when Prohibition came into effect. She and her husband began hosting cocktail parties in their apartment, and over the course of the next few years, became quite proficient in the art of covert entertaining. By the end of the decade, Virginia had teamed up with fellow host and writer Philip Duffield Strong to produce one of the most entertaining books of the period, *Shake 'Em Up: A Practical Handbook of Polite Drinking*, which they published in 1930.

Shake 'Em Up is a delightful glimpse into the customs of the cocktail party and the new social order of hosting and home entertaining that emerged during this period. The book is full of sage advice on the mixing of cocktails with sparse ingredients (hint: there's a lot of gin and juice), what to serve with them, and how to cope with the inevitable party indiscretions—from ring stains on the furniture to late, boring, or badly behaved guests. Describing the virtues of such drinks as the Grapefruit Cocktail with gin and grapefruit juice to liven up a dull crowd, Virginia wrote, "If you have invited strangers who, you just know, will like each other—and of course they don't—or if conversation languishes like a Dickens heroine, or if you don't like the party yourself, try these combinations. Repeat doses until cured."

Just like the tea party that preceded it and the happy hour tradition that followed later, the cocktail party was a gathering designed to fit the late afternoon or early evening window as a kind of pregame to later entertainments. It was an opportunity for the Apartment Hostess not only to socialize, but to get her drink on before sitting through a dry theater performance or aboveboard restaurant dinner. While writers of the time emphasized that two should be the maximum number of drinks served during an hour-long cocktail party, it's clear from Virginia and others that this rule was rarely adhered to and, far from cocktail "hour" being the precursor to the next event, it was just as likely to turn into the main event itself.

THE PROHIBITION PARLOR

Cocktail hour was an easy event for the Apartment Hostess to cater, streamlining service from her kitchenette where she would keep ice and snacks, to her corner cupboard where she kept her bar, to her coffee table and tray where she served the drinks. With no need for formal seating, anywhere from 6 to 20 guests could be comfortably accommodated for a cocktail party in a one-bedroom apartment. And for those with the luxury of hosting from a house, the cellar became the ideal venue, sometimes even decked out like the speakeasies of the day with built-in bars, comfy chairs, card tables, bar games, and Ping-Pong tables.

Curiously, unlike previous eras of grand dinners and chafing dish entertainments, food very much took a backseat during the Prohibition cocktail hour. Instead, Apartment Hostesses were advised to keep on hand simple pantry ingredients for light bites that could be pulled together at a moment's notice with minimal preparation or cleanup. This meant canapés, sandwiches, and finger foods that could be held easily in one hand while a drink was in the other. At its most basic, a Prohibition gathering was catered with canned nuts, olives, and processed spreads smeared in haste onto a cracker, celery stick, or morsel of toast.

Emphasis was now fully on the drinks, and drink recipes were borrowed not just from the old housekeeping guides, but directly from rediscovered bartending manuals that were now finding a whole new audience. For example, Virginia and Phil dedicated their book to 19th-century mixologist Jerry Thomas, and included many old bar recipes, such as the John (or Tom) Collins, Whiskey Sour, and Old-Fashioned, in their pages.

At the same time, unsurprisingly, a number of new recipes rose to popularity during this period, especially those whose flavor profiles appealed to the hostesses' tastes. Gin drinks, such as the Pink Lady, Clover Club, and Bee's Knees, were featured in women's magazines and popularized by well-known actresses and public figures of the time. One such figure was philanthropist Margaret Brown, a larger-than-life character who had become famous as a survivor of the *Titanic* disaster in 1912. Her efforts to evacuate other passengers, especially women and children, from the sinking ship had earned her the nickname in the press of "The Unsinkable Molly Brown." A decade on, it seems Margaret was equally unsinkable in her desire to keep her favorite cocktail afloat, reportedly taking the recipe for the Bee's Knees cocktail with her to Paris, where it is said she educated the bartenders of the city's women-only bars about the drink.

THE COCKTAIL COMES TO BLIGHTY

Margaret Brown was not the only hostess to move her barstool across the Atlantic during the Prohibition years. In 1925, Nina Toye, an American thriller writer living in London, cowrote a best-selling cocktail book, with cookery writer and restaurateur Alec Henry Adair, titled *Drinks: Long and Short*. Alec was the life partner of the famous French chef Marcel Boulestin, who also contributed the foreword to the book. The book was part home bartender's guide and part fanciful musing on the role of the cocktail in epicurean culture and the fine dining experience. With many classic as well as unique recipes, it was influential in Europe, published in three languages, and excerpts were widely reproduced for female readers in such British magazines as *Vogue*, *Eve*, and the *Daily Express*.

As American hostesses and writers flooded the bars and restaurants of London and Paris throughout the 1920s, it was not long before the cocktail trend started hitting the drinks scene there, too. After first rejecting the idea of "American drinks" some 20 years earlier, such British writers as Hilda Leyel, Mary Woodman, and Rose Henniker Heaton now began covering them in their own books on drinks and entertaining. In her

1925 *Summer Drinks and Winter Cordials*, botanist Hilda Leyel showed readers how to replace the oftentimes expensive or hard-to-find spirit ingredients with other more affordable liquors like wine. In *Cocktails, Ices, Sundaes, Jellies and American Drinks*, published in 1929, Mary Woodman explained how the cocktail was a dessert like treat that could be made with fruit syrups that British hostesses were otherwise using for ice cream sundaes. As Mary wrote, "A wise use of cocktails is beneficial to the health and the habit of drinking them has grown deservedly, so much so that the modern hostess should never be at a loss how to make a cocktail for the delight of her guests."

TAKING BACK CONTROL OF THE COCKTAIL

Through the temperance movement, women had first used the problem of men's drinking to solve the larger problem of equal rights. Then, as arguments for the repeal of Prohibition began to gather pace in the late 1920s and early '30s, a number of prominent women used their newfound voice and political influence to call for its reversal.

Pauline Sabin, a famous hostess to the rich and famous, political activist, and founder of the Women's Organization for National Prohibition Reform, observed how the drinking behavior of certain male politicians at private events was the opposite of what they could be heard touting in public. Drawing attention to the hypocrisy of the men in charge, she argued that a higher moral standard would prevail if drinking simply came under the direct supervision of women. Since universal adherence to temperance was now being seen as a compromise on civil liberties, and frankly a futile exercise anyway, she successfully evolved the public narrative from one of abstinence into one of responsible consumption.

The topic of respectable drinking became a strong theme with the announcement of Repeal in 1933. Virginia Elliott followed up *Shake 'Em Up* with the more phlegmatic *Quiet Drinking* that year; and on the other side of the country, journalist and veteran hostess Alma Whitaker had a similar vision that civility and decorum would prevail if only women were to take charge of the cocktail. A longtime columnist and feature writer for the *Los Angeles Times*, Alma was one of the most influential newspaper women of her age. She was also an early promoter of suffrage and had caused a stir in the lead up to Prohibition when she published an article highlighting the misogyny of societal attitudes towards women smoking.

In 1933, the year of Repeal, Alma set out her manifesto for the post-Prohibition world in *Bacchus Behave! The Lost Art of Polite Drinking*. The book is less drinks guide and more treatise on the role of the cocktail in the home. Citing the loss of decorum around drinking caused by the forbidden nature of alcohol during the Prohibition years, she argued that a successful repeal could be achieved if "the women of the nation, and specifically the hostesses, take the matter in hand," arguing, "If we are as fussy and fastidious about the quality, quantity and service of our liquor and about the conduct of our guests as we are about the food, the table service and the accouterments of our parties, all will be well." She also set out her 10 "Rules for Righteous Behavior" for the new world order, which included such sensible advice as "Never get drunk," "Never drink alone," and "Never drink when you are unhappy."

Building on her theory that women made superior hosts, Alma also recommended that women should only delegate the task of mixing drinks to the man of the house "where there is no butler to oversee the situation." For when it comes to cocktails, she wrote, "Man will be the last thing civilized by Woman."

THE SINGLE HOSTESS

However, for those women who had no husband or butler to oversee the drinks service, a new generation of Apartment Hostess was emerging in the years post-Prohibition, one who had never been seen before—the independent single woman. This woman now had the right to vote; to have some control over her fertility with expanding access to birth control; and the opportunity, if not the necessity in increasingly uncertain economic times, to participate as a meaningful part of the workforce. And with the prospect of social emancipation, economic independence, and their first taste of sexual freedom, the idea of living a single life without reference to men became not just a plausible option for women, but an attractive one, at that.

If women could live on their own terms, it stood to reason that they could host on their own terms, too. In the 1930s, prominent figures, such as *Vogue* editor Marjorie Hillis, became icons for the single life. In 1936, she published the outrageously successful best-seller *Live Alone and Like It: A Guide for the Extra Woman*, a groundbreaking text that taught women how to live by themselves and subvert the patriarchy of the drinks world. Marjorie showed her readers how to shop for liquor in stores, how to stock a bar cart, and how to serve liquor to guests at their own cocktail hours. In demystifying the cocktail, she wrote, "Buying liquor may seem like a problem in itself, but, in reality, it has ceased to be one of the great masculine mysteries. Like so many of them, it turns out to be a simple matter after all."

In 1937, Marjorie followed up *Live Alone and Like It* with the entertaining manual *Corned Beef and Caviar*, in which she jam-packed cocktail recipes alongside other party ideas for bachelorettes on a budget. Her manifesto for single life was so influential that department stores across the country comerchandised her books alongside negligees and cocktail shakers, promoting them as the ultimate capsule wardrobe for the modern single woman.

APARTMENT COCKTAILS

One of the top skills of the Apartment Hostess was knowing how to make a lot from a little at a time when ingredients were scarce, quality was questionable, and space was limited. As such, cocktailing books for the home host during the Prohibition era often focused on hacks that would keep things simple while allowing for easy variation. Out were the esoteric ingredients, complicated techniques, or unfamiliar measures that were common in old bartending manuals, and in were simplicity, creativity, and most of all, fun. As Marjorie Hillis quipped, "Whatever you do, don't let the cocktail hour be a burden. Its purpose in life is to inject a little gaiety into a weary world, and, if it doesn't do that for you, you might as well get your fun out of wearing a white ribbon and making soap-box speeches for the W.C.T.U."

When access to quality spirits could not be guaranteed, fruit juice and sugar could hide a multitude of sins, and many of the most popular recipes fell into what we would now call the sour category of cocktails. Essentially, sour cocktails follow a simple three-ingredient formula of base spirit, citrus, and sweetener in an average ratio of 2:1:1. There are four main subcategories of the sour depending on whether the drink is served short or long, whether an egg white is added to the base recipe, and/or whether a cocktail liqueur is used in place of or in addition to the sweetener.

Sour cocktails are some of the easiest and most versatile cocktails to make at home and continue to be universally crowd pleasing still today. Anyone who doesn't like lemon can try the same recipe with lime, or a whiskey drinker can try a gin recipe with a brown spirit instead, and so on. With just a little bit of tweaking the basic formula can work in countless variations.

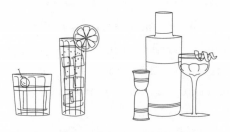

SOUR COCKTAILS

BEE'S KNEES

Makes 1 cocktail

Originally attributed to the socialite Margaret Brown in a 1929 news-paper article, the recipe for the Bee's Knees first appeared in print as an untitled cocktail in Alma Whitaker's 1933 Bacchus Behave! *Once you have the basic formula for this short sour down, you'll realize it underlies many other Prohibition era favorites, too.*

2 ounces gin
¾ ounce fresh lemon juice

½ ounce Honey Syrup
(page 37)
Garnish: lemon peel

Combine the gin, lemon juice, and honey syrup in a cocktail shaker with ice and shake to chill. Strain into a cocktail glass and roll a twist of lemon peel over the top of the drink for additional aromatics.

+ *FLAVOR INSPIRATION:*

Vary the flavor by changing the sweetener, for example Raspberry Syrup (page 37) for a Pink Lady, black-berry syrup for a Bramble, or Mint Syrup (page 38) for a Southside. Using bourbon in place of gin in the original recipe makes a drink called the Gold Rush; using lime instead of lemon makes a version known as The Business.

CLASSIC VARIATIONS

GIMLET

Makes 1 cocktail

2 ounces gin
¾ ounce fresh lime juice
½ ounce Simple Syrup
   (page 36)

Garnish: thinly sliced
lime wheel

Combine the gin, lime juice, and simple syrup in a cocktail shaker with ice and shake to chill. Strain into a cocktail glass and float a lime wheel on top of the drink.

DAIQUIRI

Makes 1 cocktail

2 ounces white rum
¾ ounce fresh lime juice
½ ounce Simple Syrup
   (page 36)

Garnish: thinly sliced
lime wheel

Combine the rum, lime juice, and simple syrup in a cocktail shaker with ice and shake to chill. Strain into a cocktail glass and float a lime wheel on top of the drink.

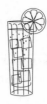

TOM COLLINS

Makes 1 cocktail

Marjorie Hillis wrote in her 1937 book Corned Beef and Caviar *that the Tom Collins is one of the best cocktails for a hostess to serve on a budget. With just three simple ingredients, it's also one of the most adaptable. Got some citrus and soda in the pantry? You've got a refreshing ready-to-drink cocktail at your fingertips.*

2 ounces gin
¾ ounce fresh lemon juice
½ ounce Simple Syrup
(page 36)

Club soda
Garnish: lemon wheel

Fill a collins glass with ice and set aside. Combine the gin, lemon juice, and syrup in a cocktail shaker, fill with additional ice, and shake quickly to blend. Strain into the collins glass and top with club soda. Garnish with the lemon wheel.

+ *FLAVOR INSPIRATION:*
For added refreshment, try infusing the simple syrup with a fresh herb, such as basil, mint, lavender, or thyme. Switching out the lemon juice for lime turns the drink into a Gin Rickey.

CLASSIC VARIATIONS

MOJITO
Makes 1 cocktail

2 ounces white rum
¾ ounce fresh lime juice
½ ounce Mint Syrup
   (page 38)

Club soda
Garnish: fresh mint

Fill a collins glass with ice and set aside. Combine the rum, lime juice, and mint syrup in a cocktail shaker, fill with additional ice, and shake quickly to blend. Strain into the collins glass and top with club soda. Garnish with mint.

PALOMA
Makes 1 cocktail

2 ounces tequila
1½ ounces grapefruit juice
½ ounce Simple Syrup
   (page 36)

Club soda
Garnish: small
   grapefruit slice

Fill a collins glass with ice and set aside. Combine the tequila, grapefruit juice, and simple syrup in a cocktail shaker, fill with additional ice, and shake quickly to blend. Strain into the collins glass and top with club soda. Garnish with the grapefruit slice.

WHISKEY SOUR

Makes 1 cocktail

Egg whites were commonly used to level out the heat of a lesser-quality spirit in Prohibition cocktails. The key to a perfectly frothy texture lies in shaking the cocktail twice. In her 1930 book Shake 'Em Up, *Virginia Elliott encourages hosts to delegate such a task to gentlemen "who have been disappointed in their youthful aspirations to become orchestra conductors or Indian Club swingers on the vaudeville stage."*

1 ounce egg white or
  aquafaba (see Note)
2 ounces whiskey
1 ounce fresh lemon juice

½ ounce Simple Syrup
  (page 36)
Garnish: maraschino cherry

Place the egg white in a tin cocktail shaker and dry shake vigorously until it's frothy and coats the sides of the tin. Add the whiskey, lemon juice, and simple syrup with ice and shake again until well chilled and foamy. Strain over fresh ice in a double old-fashioned glass or up in a cocktail glass and garnish with the maraschino cherry.

+ NOTE:
  Aquafaba (the leftover liquid in a can of chickpeas) can be used as a vegan alternative to raw egg white.

+ FLAVOR INSPIRATION:
  The frothy surface of the drink is the perfect canvas for decorating with aromatics. Try drops of aromatic bitters, grated nutmeg, or a splash of red wine to make the classic New York Sour.

CLASSIC VARIATIONS

CLOVER CLUB
Makes 1 cocktail

1 ounce egg white
  or aquafaba
2 ounces gin
1 ounce fresh lemon juice

½ ounce Raspberry Syrup
  (page 37)
Garnish: 3 fresh raspberries

Place the egg white in a tin cocktail shaker and dry shake vigorously until it's frothy and coats the sides of the tin. Add the gin, lemon juice, and raspberry syrup with ice and shake again until well chilled and foamy. Strain into a cocktail glass and garnish with the raspberries.

GIN FIZZ
Makes 1 cocktail

1 ounce egg white
  or aquafaba
2 ounces gin
1 ounce fresh lemon juice

½ ounce Simple Syrup
  (page 36)
Club soda

Fill a collins glass with ice. Place the egg white in a tin cocktail shaker and dry shake vigorously until it's frothy and coats the sides of the tin. Add the gin, lemon juice, and simple syrup to the tin with ice and shake again until well chilled and foamy. Strain into the collins glass and top with club soda.

SIDECAR

Makes 1 cocktail

While the Margarita, or tequila drinks in general, were not common in North America during Prohibition, the Margarita's great-grandmother, a sour cocktail known as the Daisy, made with gin or brandy, lemon juice, and Curaçao, certainly was (margarita being Spanish for "daisy"). So, back then it was not so much Margarita Monday or Taco Tuesday, as it was Sidecar Saturday or White Lady Wednesday.

2 ounces cognac
¾ ounce Triple Sec (page 43)
¾ ounce fresh lemon juice

¼ ounce Simple Syrup
(page 36)
Garnish: lemon twist

Combine the cognac, triple sec, lemon juice, and simple syrup in a cocktail shaker with ice and shake until thoroughly chilled. Strain over fresh ice into a rocks glass. Garnish with the lemon twist.

✛ *FLAVOR INSPIRATION:*
  For a smokier edge, try Scotch whisky as the base in this recipe, which makes a drink known as the Silent Third.

CLASSIC VARIATIONS

MARGARITA

Makes 1 cocktail

2 ounces tequila
¾ ounce Triple Sec
(page 43)

1 ounce fresh lime juice
¼ ounce Simple Syrup
(page 36)

Combine the tequila, triple sec, lime juice, and simple syrup in a cocktail shaker with ice and shake until thoroughly chilled. Strain over fresh ice into a rocks glass or up in a cocktail glass. The glass can be rimmed with salt first, if desired.

WHITE LADY

Makes 1 cocktail

2 ounces gin
¾ ounce Triple Sec
(page 43)
¾ ounce fresh lemon juice

¼ ounce Simple Syrup
(page 36)
1 ounce egg white (optional)
Garnish: lemon twist

Combine the gin, triple sec, lemon juice, and simple syrup in a cocktail shaker with ice and shake until thoroughly chilled. Strain over fresh ice into a rocks glass. Optionally, 1 ounce of egg white can be added for a creamier texture. Garnish with the lemon twist.

V

THE
GRAND
HOSTESS

c. 1940–1960

*Socializing brings people together and getting people
together promotes better understanding of common problems.*
—PERLE MESTA, 1960

In the early 20th century, Apartment Hostesses learned how to use the skill of mixing drinks as a potent weapon in their social arsenal. But by the midcentury, Grand Hostesses were taking it to another level—they were mixing *people* in the same artful way the most talented bartender mixes a perfectly balanced cocktail. Because, at its core, hosting a cocktail party is not only about providing entertainment, but also about who is in the room, and why.

Operating at the highest levels of society, Grand Hostesses of the mid-20th century used the cocktail party as a tool to stimulate social change. Unlike the Lady Hostesses of the late 19th century whose agenda was mostly driven by wealth and social status, Grand Hostesses used their influence to bring people of all backgrounds together by throwing lavish cocktail parties in grand venues all over the world with the aim of sparking conversations, inspiring diplomacy, and solving world problems.

THE HOSTESS-IN-CHIEF

There is probably no platform more prominent and no hostess more senior in the eyes of the people than that of the country's First Lady. When Prohibition was repealed in 1933, Eleanor Roosevelt had arrived in the White House, and went on to become one of the most influential First Ladies of all time. As the archetypal Grand Hostess, Eleanor took her role as the hostess-in-chief extremely seriously and is famous for using her position to highlight the needs of marginalized groups by inviting them to functions at the White House and raising their profile through her press conferences, newspaper columns, and weekly radio show. Although she, herself, was not a drinker (her father had been a severe alcoholic), neither was she a supporter of Prohibition, believing drinking should be a personal choice, and she was permissive of alcohol being served to guests at White House events even as the Volstead Act was in the process of repeal.

However, Eleanor Roosevelt was not the first First Lady to defy the law of the land around the time of Prohibition. In the years building up to the 18th Amendment, Nellie Taft had apparently ignored pressure from the Women's Christian Temperance Union demanding she refrain from serving her famous Champagne punch at White House events while her husband, William Taft, was president. And later when he was appointed chief justice of the United States Supreme Court and enforcer of the Volstead Act, she reportedly violated his rule of law by accepting alcohol wherever it was being served.

Similarly, Edith Wilson, who was First Lady to Woodrow Wilson when the Volstead Act was passed in 1919, was well known for openly serving alcohol to guests at her private home in Washington, DC. Florence Harding, who succeeded Edith in 1921 when Warren Harding became president, was rumored to be the unofficial bartender for her husband when he entertained guests privately in the Oval Office during the early years of Prohibition. As the cocktail went mainstream in the decades following Prohibition, successive First Ladies in the midcentury would become famous for their cocktail predilections, such as Bess Truman with her Old-Fashioneds, Mamie Eisenhower and her Manhattans, and Jackie Kennedy's love of all things Champagne.

That First Ladies have historically contributed cocktails to the White House bar is well documented in such books as *Housekeeping in Old Virginia: Containing Contributions from 250 of Virginia's Noted Housewives*, by Marion Cabell Tyree, published in 1879, and the *White House Cook Book*, published by Fanny Lemira Gillette in 1887. The books attribute various commonly served drinks, such as Champagne punch, to the wives of presidents, senators, and governors and reveal the menus of real-life White House dinners where they were served. Indeed, Champagne punch was said to be so popular at the White House that it continued to be served customarily at dinners well into the second half of the 20th century.

THE HOSTESS WITH THE MOSTES'

When First Ladies were not doing the entertaining, they were often the ones being entertained, and there was no greater entertainer and Grand Hostess of the post-Prohibition era than Perle Mesta. Perle was the eldest daughter of an Oklahoman oil and real estate tycoon who had built one of the most iconic hotels in the state, the Skirvin Hotel in Oklahoma City. Brought up in her father's world of hospitality, Perle reportedly threw her first party at the hotel at the age of 11, entertaining her prepubescent guests with nasturtium sandwiches and a Japanese lantern show.

In 1925, the recently widowed Perle moved into the Barclay Hotel in New York City, where she began holding lavish galas for the "Met-Set," entertaining the upper-class regulars of the Metropolitan Opera with Champagne and cocktail parties. By the 1940s, she had established herself as the ultimate party host. Throughout the midcentury, Perle's cocktail parties would bring together government officials, diplomats, executives, philanthropists, and artists in extravagant bashes stretching from Washington, DC, to New York, London, and Hollywood.

Despite her high position in society, however, Perle did not invite guests to her parties based on their place on the social register. Instead, her number one rule for a great party was to "like the people you invite and make every one of your guests feel wanted." She invited people "in the thick of things" who she felt needed to meet, which included "big wigs, little wigs, and no wigs at all." Neither did she shy away from bringing controversial figures who would never normally be seen in public together. In Perle's grand parlor, the convivial atmosphere, good food, music, and cocktails made differences of opinion and matters of policy easier to resolve.

Importantly, Perle also believed that the presence of women at such gatherings brought a savoir-faire to the conversation that was missing from the male-dominated boardrooms and policy-making assembly halls of the time. At a time when women had no seat at the table, she ensured their voices would be heard in the most direct, spontaneous, and unfiltered way possible—that is, over a good cocktail.

Such was Perle's influence and ability to resolve conflict that, in 1949, she was called up by the State Department to serve as the United States' first ambassador to Luxembourg, simultaneously becoming the nation's first-ever female ambassador. She brought the same sensibility to her diplomatic post as she did to her social role. As she later reflected in her memoir, *Perle: My Story,* "Somehow, I wondered why our Foreign Service always insisted that the job of diplomacy be done only at the top levels where tradition and protocol turn it into coldly formal and uninspired negotiations. It seems to me this is the opposite of everything America stands for as a nation. Diplomacy based on simple dignity, on informality, on warm and neighborly greeting would appear to be not only more desirable but more effective." A sentiment that might sound more recognizable coming from a friendly neighborhood bartender than it would from a prominent state official.

It's also true to say that Perle left an indelible mark on the cocktail. Every event she held started with a cocktail hour and she ensured that the Champagne would continue to flow liberally throughout the evening. Her closest aide and chief of staff, Garner Camper, was personally tasked with remembering the names and drink preferences of all her guests, which would have numbered in the many thousands over the years. And as if that weren't enough, legend has it that, in 1949, a bartender at the Hotel Metropole in Brussels created an infamous vodka and coffee cocktail, called the Black Russian, in honor of Perle when she was a guest at the hotel.

Immortalized by the moniker "The Hostess with the Mostes'" by Irving Berlin in his 1950 Broadway musical *Call Me Madam,* Perle embodied the gold standard for Grand Hostesses everywhere.

THE GREAT SALONKEEPERS

Perle Mesta was not the only Grand Hostess renowned for her audiences with the rich and famous during the 1940s and '50s. She had stiff competition from an archrival, Elsa Maxwell, who dubbed herself "The Queen of Party Givers." Like Perle, Elsa had been throwing parties since the age of 12 and had made a professional career of it, publishing her tips in 1957 in a book titled *How to Do It: Or the Lively Art of Entertaining.* While Elsa herself claimed in later years to be teetotal, her cocktail parties were nevertheless legendary. For example, at one of her glittering galas, she famously greeted every female guest on arrival with a cocktail matching the color of the guest's dress.

Another Grand Hostess who held nightly soirees in her Manhattan parlor during this time was Clara Bell Walsh, the same progressive who had previously gained notoriety for first inventing the cocktail party back in 1917. As a resident of the luxury Plaza Hotel in New York City, she brought a cornucopia of visitors into her afternoon salons in her apartment, ranging from Broadway actors and actresses to world-famous wrestlers, politicians, and a great number of prominent civil rights figures. An independently wealthy divorcée, and a daily drinker of Kentucky Old-Fashioneds, at night she would throw legendary parties with upward 200 guests, leading her to describe herself later in life as "the last of the salonkeepers."

After the years of clandestine cocktail parties during the 1920s and '30s, Perle Mesta, Elsa Maxwell, Clara Walsh, and other Grand Hostesses brought the cocktail party to the highest of levels and set the stage for it to become the model for grand entertaining in America in the second half of the century. As Elsa proclaimed in *The Lively Art of Entertaining*, "When a congressman wants to be put on record by the press, when a cosmetics firm wants to introduce a new lipstick, when Marilyn Monroe wants to announce herself incorporated to the greater glory of Dostoevsky, a cocktail party is the obvious means," and the formal cocktail party is arguably the most effective way to make a splash with a large and/or high-profile audience still to this day.

THE JOY GODDESS OF HARLEM

Farther uptown in New York City, A'Lelia Walker, the daughter of entrepreneur Madam C. J. Walker, the first self-made woman and African American millionaire, held court at cocktail parties attended by some of the most famous figures during the Harlem Renaissance era. In the 1920s, she famously converted a floor of her Harlem town house into the Dark Tower, a literary salon, nightclub, and tearoom that became a legendary hot spot for Black writers, artists, and performers, attracting prominent publishers, civil rights leaders, and even African and European royalty as its guests. The tower was open until two a.m., cost $1 to join, and was always thronging. According to poet Langston Hughes, "Unless you went early there was no possible way of getting in. Her parties were as crowded as the New York subway at the rush hour—entrance, lobby, steps, hallway, and apartment a milling crush of guests, with everybody seeming to enjoy the crowding."

Langston Hughes dubbed A'Lelia the "Joy Goddess of Harlem" because of how she brought people together with lavish food, sparkling drinks, and music from the top classical, ragtime, jazz, and blues artists of the day. However, like other Grand Hostesses, A'Lelia was not only a celebrated hostess, but also a prominent social activist. In particular, her events were known as safe spaces for the LGBTQ community at a time when being Black and gay was virtually a social impossibility. As the dancer and former guest Mabel Hamilton once recalled, "There were men and women, women and women, and men and men, and everyone did whatever they wanted to do."

A'Lelia's parties were some of the most hotly attended and widely reported gatherings of the Harlem Renaissance era. One of the journalists who reported on her events was Geraldyn Dismond. A familiar and glamorous figure in the scene, she was known locally as "Harlem's Hostess." In the 1930s, she wrote a syndicated column called "The Social Whirl" in which she reported on social happenings and shared cocktail and hosting tips. In one article she revealed her own signature cocktail to be the Green Skirt, which she made with two-thirds gin, one-third crème de menthe, a dash of lemon juice, and a minted cherry, served over crushed ice.

Geraldyn, or Gerri Major as she was otherwise known, would continue to influence Black media and cocktail culture for decades to come as associate editor of *Jet* magazine and later senior staff editor of *Ebony* magazine.

GRAND DRINKING PARLORS

During the early 20th century, the venues for cocktail parties got a major makeover when women began entering the field of professional interior design. One of the most influential designers of the period was Elsie de Wolfe, whose trademark style of pastel and chintz transformed the dark and dull reception rooms of the Victorian era into the bright, cheerful, and feminine parlors that became the venues for the first cocktail parties in the 1920s and '30s.

Elsie was said to be a legendary hostess, herself, and like other Grand Hostesses of the era, gave parties usually attended by the chicest members of society. One of her regular guests was the infamous Wallis Simpson, Duchess of Windsor, who once remarked of her host, "She mixes people like a cocktail—and the result is sheer genius." In the 1920s, *Vogue* shared a recipe for Elsie's signature drink served at her parties, known as Lady Mendl's Invention. The drink was composed of gin, grenadine, lemon, and egg white, which led many at the time to speculate that Elsie was the creator of the original Pink Lady cocktail.

Another high-profile designer of the midcentury era was Dorothy Draper, whose bold feminine designs transformed some of the most iconic hotels and restaurants in the country, including the Greenbrier Resort in West Virginia, the Fairmont Hotel in San Francisco, the Beverly Hills Hotel in Los Angeles, the Plaza Hotel in New York City, and the Mayflower Hotel in Washington, DC.

Dorothy had a deep understanding of how people, and especially women, wanted to feel when they were drinking a cocktail, and brought this sentiment forward into her designs. For example, one of her well-known commissions was the Camellia House Supper Club at the Drake Hotel in Chicago, where she famously used a bright pink camellia motif in every aspect of the space, from the carpets and light fixtures of the lounge to the matchbook covers and swizzle sticks of the bar. The overall effect was bold, feminine, flirty, and chic—a stark contrast to the dark, austere, and masculine hotel bars and private clubs where the cocktail had first got its start.

As Dorothy's influence spread to a wide audience through the 1940s and '50s via her books, magazine columns, and branded line of home decor and furniture, her ideas would help transform the living rooms of suburban America into the venues for the mainstream cocktail parties that dominated suburban life in the '50s and '60s. In 1941, she published her own entertaining guide, *Entertaining Is Fun! How to Be a Popular Hostess*, in which she described the feeling that the midcentury cocktail parlor should invoke, writing: "This begins when your guests reach the living room. There they should get the glamour feeling of the tall white candles in silver or glass candlesticks that have been lighted before the arrival of the first guest; the open fire blazing cheerily on the hearth, the flowers . . . the little table with the decanter of sherry, the glasses and plate of plain biscuits or simple but delicious canapés, the cocktails, shaken up and ready to be poured *at once*."

Dorothy was one of the most influential hostesses to stress the importance of the ambience of the home parlor to the overall experience of the cocktail. As she concluded, "There isn't anyone who can walk onto a stage-set like that without involuntarily stopping to exclaim, 'But how lovely!' And that, of course, is just what you want."

GRAND COCKTAILS

The ultimate aim of the Grand Hostesses was to use lavish cocktail soirees to inspire conviviality; and the lesson from the menus of these hostesses is that the liquid denominator of any fancy event, regardless of time, geography, or occasion, is Champagne. Nothing says pomp and ceremony like the popping of the cork, and still to this day, a Champagne cocktail remains the hero on all of the most celebratory cocktail occasions. And like First Lady Nellie Taft, whose Champagne punch was said to include a multitude of other liquor ingredients; Fanny Gillette, whose White House–inspired recipe was designed to be served over fresh snow; or Perle Mesta, who once famously covered her whole apartment with a Champagne and orchid theme, the modern hostess knows that Champagne cocktails should always be top of the menu when a standout celebration is called for.

It should also be pointed out that serving a Champagne cocktail is, itself, an act of recognition of women. Unlike other areas of wine and spirits that have been historically woefully male dominated, Champagne has had many female leaders, and in particular, the "Grandes Dames," or widows, of Champagne. Women like Barbe-Nicole Ponsardin of Veuve Clicquot; Louise Pommery, of Pommery; Marie-Louise Lanson de Nonancourt, of Laurent-Perrier; Apolline Henriot, of Henriot; Lily Bollinger, of Bollinger; and their descendants, have been the driving force of the industry for over two centuries.

Similarly, the coupe, the original Champagne glass that became the standard vessel for many cocktails, has a decidedly feminine history. Legend has it that the shape of the bowl was first modeled on the breasts of Marie Antoinette, the wife of Louis XVI of France, although other famous breasts have also laid claim to the title, including Madame de Pompadour, mistress of Louis XV of France; Josephine, wife of Napoléon Bonaparte; and Helen of Troy.

The following recipes are a selection of classic Champagne cocktails that will never fail to make an occasion feel special. While the additional ingredients used in these recipes are quite modest, for those on a budget or for whom the thought of using good Champagne as a cocktail mixer is either a sacrilege or an unnecessary luxury, dry sparkling wines, such as Reserva or Gran Reserva Cava, from Spain; DOCG Prosecco, from Italy; Crémant from France; or Brut wines, from the United States, make perfectly good alternatives.

SPARKLING COCKTAILS

CHAMPAGNE COCKTAIL

Makes 1 cocktail

Probably one of the most elegant of all cocktails, the Champagne Cocktail was a favorite welcome drink of such Grand Hostesses as Perle Mesta and Elsa Maxwell. Essentially an Old-Fashioned in Champagne form, the traditional recipe calls for use of a sugar cube, which as it dissolves makes the drink taste pleasingly sweeter and more flavorful the further you work your way down.

1 sugar cube, or ½ ounce
    Simple Syrup (page 36)
3 to 5 dashes
    aromatic bitters

4 to 5 ounces
    Champagne, chilled
Garnish: lemon twist

Place the sugar cube in the bottom of a Champagne flute and saturate with the bitters. Slowly pour the Champagne on top of the sugar cube to fill the glass, and garnish with the lemon twist.

+ *FLAVOR INSPIRATION:*
   It's hard to improve on this classic, but changing out the bitters or using fancily infused sugar cubes can be a treat for a special occasion.

FRENCH 75

Makes 1 cocktail

Named in France for the lethal gun used during the First World War—the Soixante-Quinze—the French 75 was once described by British novelist Alec Waugh as "the most powerful drink in the world." Certainly, the spirit and wine combination delivers a punch, so best to proceed with caution if serving up more than one round.

1 ounce gin
½ ounce fresh lemon juice
½ ounce Simple Syrup
   (page 36)

3 ounces Champagne,
   chilled
Garnish: lemon twist

Combine the gin, lemon juice, and simple syrup in a cocktail shaker with ice and shake until well chilled. Strain into a Champagne flute and top with the chilled Champagne. Garnish with the lemon twist.

✦ *FLAVOR INSPIRATION:*
   As with the Tom Collins, this cocktail can be elevated with a simple syrup infusion or by muddling some fruit into the liquors. Try muddled cucumber and infused lavender syrup in the summer, or whole cranberries and Raspberry Syrup (page 37) in the winter.

CLASSIC VARIATIONS

FRENCH 125
Makes 1 cocktail

1 ounce cognac
½ ounce fresh lemon juice
½ ounce Simple Syrup
    (page 36)

3 ounces Champagne,
    chilled
Garnish: lemon twist

Combine the cognac, lemon juice, and simple syrup in a cocktail shaker with ice and shake until well chilled. Strain into a Champagne flute and top with the chilled Champagne. Garnish with the lemon twist.

OLD CUBAN
Makes 1 cocktail

1½ ounces rum
¾ ounce fresh lime juice
1 ounce Mint Syrup
    (page 38)

Dash of aromatic bitters
2 ounces Champagne,
    chilled
Garnish: fresh mint

Combine the rum, lime juice, mint syrup, and bitters in a cocktail shaker with ice and shake until well chilled. Strain into a coupe glass and top with the chilled Champagne. Garnish with the mint.

+ *NOTE:*

A mix of rums works well in this recipe; try 1 ounce of white rum with ½ ounce of dark rum.

KIR ROYALE

Makes 1 cocktail

When Jacqueline Lee Bouvier Kennedy was serving as First Lady, she was famous for bringing chic continental style to White House–hosted events. And so, it should be no surprise to learn that the Kir Royale, an aperitif cocktail originally hailing from France, has been de rigueur in America since around the same time.

½ ounce crème de cassis
4 to 5 ounces
   Champagne, chilled

Garnish: fresh raspberry or
   lemon twist

Pour the crème de cassis into a Champagne flute and fill slowly with the chilled Champagne. Garnish with the raspberry or lemon twist.

✦ *FLAVOR INSPIRATION:*
In barspeak, to "royale" a cocktail means to add sparkling wine, and this recipe can be easily made with whatever fruit liqueurs you have lurking at the back of your home bar. Try raspberry, apricot, melon, or pear and see which is your favorite.

CLASSIC VARIATION

GRAND ROYALE

Makes 1 cocktail

½ ounce Curaçao
   (page 42)

4 to 5 ounces
   Champagne, chilled
Garnish: orange twist

Pour the Curaçao into a Champagne flute and fill slowly with the chilled Champagne. Garnish with the orange twist.

MIMOSA

Makes 1 cocktail

In Great Britain, the quintessential mix of orange juice and champagne is called a Buck's Fizz, while in the United States, it's better known as a Mimosa. During the midcentury, Grand Hostesses on both sides of the pond liked to serve them at morning celebrations or as a kickoff to daytime events, such as weddings.

2 ounces fresh orange juice, chilled	3 ounces Champagne, chilled

Pour the orange juice into a champagne flute and top slowly with the champagne.

+ *FLAVOR INSPIRATION:*
   Any citrus or tropical fruit juice works well in a Mimosa. Depending on what's in season, try blood orange or pink grapefruit in the spring, or clementine and mandarin in the fall and winter.

CLASSIC VARIATIONS

BELLINI
Makes 1 cocktail

2 ounces peach
nectar, chilled

3 ounces chilled Prosecco

Pour the peach nectar into a Champagne flute and top slowly with the
Prosecco.

ROSSINI
Makes 1 cocktail

1 ounce strawberry
puree, chilled

4 ounces chilled Prosecco

Pour the strawberry purée into a Champagne flute and top slowly with
the Prosecco.

VI

THE
SUBURBAN
HOSTESS

c. 1950–1970

At cocktail time the atmosphere is charged with the same
excitement found in a good adventure story at the point
where something mysterious or unknown is about to happen.
—CAROLYN COGGINS, 1952

By the time the 1950s rolled around, the cocktail party had become *the* blueprint for home entertaining across the United States. Not only for the large receptions of the Grand Hostesses, or for the covert city gatherings of the Apartment Hostesses, the cocktail party was now also in vogue for every Suburban Hostess. And with it the cocktail became a globally recognized symbol of American hospitality and style.

This entertaining revolution was catalyzed by several interrelated socio-economic trends during the 1950s. After a long period of austerity brought about by the Great Depression and Second World War in the '30s and '40s, the combination of an economic boom, a baby boom, and a housing boom caused the mass exodus of American middle-class families from city centers to the suburbs. And with this move came a renewed focus on the nuclear family. Women, who had fought for so long for economic and social independence in the early part of the century, suddenly found themselves back in an ideological framework that centered squarely on the home. In the '50s, even if a woman worked in a job outside the home—as 1 in 3 of them did—her contribution to society was publicly measured in terms of her role as wife, mother, cook, housekeeper, and crucially, hostess.

The Suburban Hostess was represented in popular culture as the gracious wife in an ever state of readiness to welcome her husband, his work colleagues, and their friends and neighbors into her living room with a perfectly lipsticked smile and an even more perfectly chilled drink. So, how did this new generation of Suburban Hostess run the party while simultaneously being the life of the party? The answer was, by throwing a cocktail party.

COCKTAILS MAKETH THE WOMAN

The cocktail party was a cultural phenomenon that captured the mood of the nation in the 1950s. Since the days of Prohibition, the cocktail had come to stand for America's sense of progressive ingenuity, a symbol of her ability to make something out of nothing, to be resilient in the face of hardship, and to bring people together in both the darkest and the lightest of times. For many, it was an icon for hospitality itself. Midcentury writer Carolyn Coggins described the cocktail as "ready hospitality" because of the way it could engender a warm, convivial atmosphere with just one clink of the glass. With a cocktail in hand, anything could happen.

Carolyn was arguably one of the most accomplished and prominent cocktail party architects of her time. As a highly influential literary editor and book journalist in the United States during the 1930s and '40s, she had spent years flying across the country, profiling authors, surveying bookstores, and mingling with the literary glitterati at nightly cocktail soirees. After deciding on a career change in the late '40s, she flew to Paris to study French cooking at Le Cordon Bleu school, and when she returned home, wrote multiple cookbooks, later teaching courses on elevated French cuisine right around the time that a certain Julia Child was also beginning her rise to fame.

When Carolyn's hosting book *Successful Entertaining at Home* was published in 1952, it was an instant best seller and syndicated into a six-week newspaper series that ran in outlets across the country. In the chapter titled "More Fun Than Food," she explored the taxonomy of the American cocktail party. For example, she described cocktail parties that would start at 6 p.m. in the midweek, those that began at 4 p.m. on weekends, and others that started at 10 p.m. such as the after-theater cocktail party. She talked about cocktail parties with no food, those with substantial food but no dinner, the mixed tea and cocktail party, the dessert cocktail party, and the cocktail buffet party. And she described different party styles and occasions, from the small neighborly cocktail parties to the spontaneous get togethers, formal corporate networking events, and large cocktail parties for special occasions.

Name the type of social event in the 1950s, and it seemed there was a cocktail party style to fit the bill.

DRINKS BEFORE FOOD

The most consistent feature of a cocktail party was its length (around two hours) and focus on drinks and conversation rather than on fine dining. The relaxed informality of the occasion was liberating for the Suburban Hostess, especially when compared to the lengthy staged dinners of previous generations. Being a skilled cook was not a prerequisite for hosting a good cocktail party, and in fact, serving food of any kind was somewhat optional. As Carolyn explained, "The cocktail party came first, gradually being combined with food in various ways and at various hours." Nevertheless, most people did serve some kind of food at their parties, and the gastronomy that emerged from the cocktail party would go on to become a culinary art form in its own right.

If the tea party of the 1910s was the era of the sandwich, then it's safe to say that the appetizer came of age during the cocktail parties of the 1950s. Scores of cocktail books such as *Party Food and Drink* by Rosemary Hume; *Cocktail Snacks and Canapés* by Mollie Stanley-Wrench; and *Cocktail Companions: Snacks for all Occasions* by Marian Courtney, published over the decade covered the cornucopia of finger foods and snack options that could be rustled up by an inventive hostess to soak up the libations of a thirsty crowd. Everything from dips to pick-up-sticks, spreads, rolls, puffs, poufs, balls, wheels, cubes, rings, bites, and wedges would be piled high onto side tables, passed around on doily-covered plates, and arranged on the family dining table, now pushed back against the wall to aid the free-flowing movement of drinking guests.

For the more ambitious hostess, the smorgasbord of snacks would give way to a full-blown buffet composed of chafing dishes and platters in service of a multicourse meal. One such popularizer of this cocktail buffet supper was Marion Flexnor, a Kentucky-based food writer and contributor to fashionable women's magazines, such as *Vogue*, *Woman's Day*, and *House and Garden*. Marion's mother was famous 19th-century author Adele Kahn Weil—also known as "Miss Adele"—who had previously written about wine cups and other boozy drinks for the

Lady Hostess in *The Twentieth Century Cook Book* in 1898. In 1955, daughter Marion published the *Cocktail Supper Cook-Book*, in which she laid out 50 menus and over 300 recipes for themed buffets from around the world, each of which centered on an opening cocktail. For example, her "California Here We Come" menu featured the Moscow Mule with cracked crabs and caraway breadsticks, while her "Fabulous Philadelphia" menu paired a rye Old-Fashioned with Philadelphia pepper pot and strawberry dream cake.

Suburban Hostesses like Marion used the cocktail party to break away from centuries of formal dining etiquette and open the door to a more relaxed, playful and personal style of entertaining that was accessible to any host, regardless of age or social background.

THE LIVING ROOM IS THE NEW PARLOR

With the living room now the focal point of entertaining in the suburban home, and the cocktail the focal point of the entertainment, the form and function of the American parlor also began to evolve. In *Successful Entertaining at Home*, Carolyn Coggins idealized a new modern living space that was "sufficiently adept (and supplied) to entertain a dozen people for cocktails at an hour's notice, without a maid, at the end of a busy day at the office."

The centerpiece of this midcentury living room was the bar—not so much a commercial-style bar, which Carolyn felt to be tacky and obtrusive; rather, a bar cart, side table, or chest, usually located behind a sofa, and staged at all times with an ice bucket, decanters, tongs, coasters, and napkins. On a wall near the bar would be a cabinet with one of its shelves dedicated to glassware, one to mixers, and a third to the standard six-bottle bar, which at this time included Scotch whisky, American whiskey, rum, gin, bitters, and vermouth. A plentiful supply of cigarettes, matches, and ashtrays or bowls were the finishing touch to a living room that was always party-ready.

Keeping alcohol, specifically spirits and their associated accoutrements, on display in the main living area of the house was a status symbol that reflected how liquor had become an important form of social currency in the 1950s. For example, the tradition of offering a bottle of liquor as a hostess gift, which had first started during the thrifty Prohibition years, became widespread during this period, as did the practices of giving alcohol as holiday gifts, and barware as engagement or wedding gifts. Furniture pieces for the living room that were inspired by or dedicated to the cocktail—such as the glassware cabinet, the cocktail table, and the bar cart—were also widely marketed in magazines and department store catalogs during this period. In fact, the cocktail had become so iconic in design and culture in America that, in a 1958 article about the future of aerospace engineering that featured an idea for a martini glass–shaped spacecraft, the *New York Times* declared the vessel to be "the symbol of our civilization."

THE DIVISION OF PARTY LABOR

Alongside the bar cart, a phonograph for long-playing records also became a fixture of the modern living room during the midcentury, and the job of mixing drinks and selecting music at a cocktail party was commonly delegated by the Suburban Hostess to her male cohost or guest. As socialite Maureen Daly wrote in her book *The Perfect Hostess* in 1950, "If you have an especially close male friend on the guest list—one who's a good amateur bartender—ask him to help mix drinks in the kitchen. He'll be delighted, and it will simplify things if he mixes and you serve." Alternatively, she suggested, "you might put all the ingredients for the cocktails on an attractive tray, set it on a side table or a large coffee table—and let the guests mix their own. The male guests will serve the girls, and everything will get to be very cozy."

This gendered division of labor between food and drink at a cocktail party became the norm in the fifties and was also reflected in several popular cocktail books written by husband-wife partnerships during this time. One example was the 1958 book by Helen Evans Brown, a well-known Californian chef and writer, called *A Book of Appetizers*. To accompany her appetizer recipes, she invited her husband, Philip, who was also her chief taste-tester and typing assistant, to contribute a hundred of his own favorite cocktail recipes to the book.

Another food writer, Anne London, who was director of the Home-makers Research Institute, published *Cocktails and Snacks* with Robert London in 1953. Described in the foreword as "a bartender's guide and a cookbook for people who get fun and pleasure out of life by entertaining—who take their bars, pantries, and kitchens seriously," the book contained several hundred cocktail recipes contributed by Robert, with almost as many snacks devised by Anne. The book was widely successful, and fully revised and expanded to more than 1,250 recipes in 1965. In one review of the second edition, it was described as "the last word" on the cocktail party and "as complete a collection as could be found." With this book as a guide, the reviewer went on to say, "no hostess could help but be a successful party giver."

Both Anne and Helen already had successful careers as food writers at the time they wrote these books about cocktails. However, by teaming up with male partners to create these comprehensive guides, they effectively brought cocktail party cuisine to a wide audience of both men *and* women.

PRETTY FOR THE PARTY

The aforementioned writer Maureen Daly first shot to fame in 1942, when her teenage novel, *Seventeenth Summer*, became a national best seller, selling over a million copies and kicking off a new category of fiction that would later become known as the Young Adult genre. Together with her sisters Maggie, Kay, and Sheila John, the "Daly sisters" were the influencers of the 1950s. Young, beautiful, and highly successful in their respective worlds of media, fashion, and advertising, they were the poster children for the aspirational white working woman and featured frequently in such high-profile magazines as *Life* and *Time*.

In 1950, the newly married Maureen published a lifestyle book titled *The Perfect Hostess*, aimed at what she called the "new generation" of working married women and single career girls. In addition to cocktail making advice and boy-girl party etiquette, she also notably included a 30-minute beauty routine to help the aspiring hostess get party-ready. Warning her readers about the perils of neglecting this one important step, she wrote, "Have you ever been to a party at which the food was fabulous, the house looked heavenly—and the hostess looked like a lady who had recently been through a wringer? This can happen, you know. And it can happen to you, whether you are a career-girl or wife, if you don't include yourself in the preparty 'prettying-up' process."

The idea that the hostess was an important part of the scenery of the cocktail party was a common refrain among commentators during this period. Television and radio personality Charlotte Adams, another famous etiquette guru, published her best-selling cocktail party guide *Home Entertaining*, also in 1950. Described in the marketing as "an encyclopedia of hospitality," the book's topics ranged from party planning to food, drinks, and party games. Like Maureen, Charlotte came from a fashion family (her sister, Elizabeth Hawes, was a well-known fashion designer) and her book similarly included a good deal of advice on how the modern hostess should gussy up for her parties. Whereas Maureen's secret was the makeup routine, Charlotte's lay in the power of the wardrobe, and in particular, the little black dress. As she advised, "If you only have one evening dress, your best choice of color is black. People don't remember they've seen you in it again and again as they do a frock of an unforgettable color."

The origin of the little black dress, or L.B.D., dates back to 1926, when up-and-coming Parisian designer Gabrielle "Coco" Chanel introduced a short black evening sheath dress to the readers of *Vogue* magazine, causing a global sensation. Designed to transition the wearer effortlessly from day to evening, the L.B.D. ushered in a new paradigm in the way women would dress and socialize at cocktail hour. Dressing up for drinks became a style in its own right from the 1920s onward, and the cocktail dress a staple of every woman's wardrobe for most of the 20th century.

The popularity of the cocktail dress reached its peak in 1954, when fashion designer Christian Dior added the term "cocktail dress" to his *Little Dictionary of Fashion*. In his 1957 autobiography, *Dior on Dior*, he went on to say, "The real masterpiece of American design are the cocktail dresses, the cocktail being the symbol par excellence of the American way of life." Dior's signature New Look, with its cinched waist, full skirt, ornamental neckline, and elaborate trimmings, became a defining image of the 1950s, and the silhouette was heavily promoted on the runways, in movies and fashion magazines, and all across suburban department stores.

Key to the cocktail look were the accessories, which included such items as cocktail hats, cocktail gloves, and bright, eye-catching cocktail jewelry. Even today, cocktail jewelry is the hallmark of the day-to-night transitional style. The centerpiece of this look is arguably the cocktail ring, which first appeared on the fingers of cocktail-drinking fashionistas during the speakeasy parties of the 1920s. Ostentatious, colorful, and often exorbitantly expensive, the original purpose of the cocktail ring was to draw attention to what was in the hand—that is, the cocktail— and was considered a subversive act by women alongside the short hairstyles and hemlines of the Flapper era. Cocktail rings and other types of statement jewelry exploded in popularity again in the midcentury, not as a political statement this time, but as symbols of the booming economy and the new trend in conspicuous consumerism.

By bringing the cocktail into fashion and making the ritual an occasion worth dressing up for, the hostesses of this period turned cocktail style into something glamorous and aspirational. And while day-to-night fashion has clearly changed many times in the decades since, the cultural resonance of the cocktail and, of cocktail style more generally, has remained. Today, when a host or hostess calls for "cocktail attire" at an event, it is not so much to indicate a certain beverage menu, as it is to send a message to their guests that they should expect the setting, menu, dress code, and tone to be playful, fancy, elegant, and fun.

SUBURBAN COCKTAILS

In her book on hosting, socialite Maureen Daly wrote, "At most cocktail parties, you'll find that guests prefer Martinis, Manhattans, Old-Fashioneds or sherry," saying, "happily, you can serve them to even the snootiest drinkers, since they are the most popular cocktails." A far cry from the inventive and diverse drinks of the pre-Prohibition era, the 1950s Suburban Hostesses returned to these old standbys because they were simple to manage, widely popular, and required little in the way of expertise to mix. In fact, almost all hosting books from this era focus on the holy cocktail trinity of the Martini, Manhattan, and Old-Fashioned as the drinks to always keep on menu for the suburban cocktail hour.

Outside of the classic stirred drinks, however, tiki drinks and rum-based cocktails also gained popularity during this time, especially in the bars and restaurants of the larger cities. The interest in tropical drinks was a direct result of the development of the airline industry in the 1950s, which had led to a boom in tourism to exotic destinations like the new state of Hawaii, Mexico, the Caribbean, and Central America. As a result, food and drinks that American tourists were experiencing on vacation were finding their way onto restaurant and bar menus back home in the United States. Such drinks as the Daiquiri, Piña Colada, Zombie, and Mai Tai were popular in bars and also made appearances in several of the more expansive home guides of the time, alongside simpler rum-based mixtures; for instance, the Cuba Libre and Bacardi cocktail.

In addition to exotic food and drink, many American hosts were also developing an appreciation for regional cuisines during this time. Such writers as Freda DeKnight, the food editor of *Ebony* magazine (and the first-ever Black food editor in the United States), and previously discussed West Coast chef Helen Evans Brown, wrote best-selling books that celebrated the multinational roots of American cuisine. For example, Helen showcased Mexican influences on southwestern food, while Freda aimed to elevate African American cooking for the middle-class Black consumer. Her 1948 *A Date with a Dish: A Cookbook of American Negro Recipes* is still considered one of the most influential books on food and drink to be published by a Black author, and her chapter on beverages included many unique alcoholic and nonalcoholic recipes that were not found in other books of the period.

All this being said, if you were living in the suburbs and hosting a cocktail party in America in the 1950s, the chances are that you were serving highballs and the classic stirred drinks—fail-safes that have stood the test of time and are regulars on cocktail menus even today. Although tastes and preferences have invariably changed in the years since these recipes were published, the specifications that follow are reflective of the way these drinks were most commonly served at cocktail hour during this era.

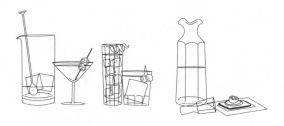

STIRRED COCKTAILS

MARTINI

Makes 1 cocktail

The Martini was so ubiquitous at midcentury cocktail parties that writers like Carolyn Coggins often advised hostesses to keep a premixed decanter of it ready in their living rooms for service at short notice. Despite being essentially a two-ingredient cocktail, the Martini tends to stir up a lot of arguments about how it should be mixed. Yet from 1950s hosting records, it seems our grandmothers were mostly serving them like this.

2 ounces gin
¾ ounce dry vermouth

Garnish: green olive or
lemon twist

Combine the gin and vermouth in a mixing glass with ice and stir until chilled. Strain into a chilled cocktail glass and garnish with the green olive or lemon twist.

+ *FLAVOR INSPIRATION:*
  A dash of orange or aromatic bitters can be added to lend further botanical depth. Changing out the green olive for a pickled onion makes a variation known as the Gibson.

CLASSIC VARIATIONS

PERFECT MARTINI
Makes 1 cocktail

1½ ounces gin
¾ ounce dry vermouth

¾ ounce sweet vermouth
Garnish: orange twist

Combine the gin, dry vermouth, and sweet vermouth in a mixing glass with ice and stir until chilled. Strain into a chilled cocktail glass and garnish with the orange twist.

SWEET MARTINI
Makes 1 cocktail

2 ounces gin
¾ ounce sweet vermouth

Garnish: maraschino cherry

Combine the gin and sweet vermouth in a mixing glass with ice and stir until chilled. Strain into a chilled cocktail glass and garnish with the maraschino cherry.

MANHATTAN

Makes 1 cocktail

The Manhattan has been a staple of American predinner drinking for over a century. Being a New York cocktail in origin, the traditional preference has been for a rye base, although any barrel-aged spirit can technically be used. Indeed, in their 1953 Cocktails and Snacks, *Anne and Robert London describe at least seven different kinds of Manhattan, as well as a Manhattan canapé made with egg, capers, and caviar and served on toast.*

2 ounces rye	2 dashes aromatic bitters
1 ounce sweet vermouth	Garnish: maraschino cherry

Combine the rye, vermouth, and bitters in a mixing glass with ice and stir until chilled. Strain into a chilled cocktail glass and garnish with the maraschino cherry.

+ *FLAVOR INSPIRATION:*
  You can have fun changing out the bitters in this recipe. Try cherry, coffee, chocolate, or walnut. When made with Scotch, this cocktail is known as a Rob Roy.

CLASSIC VARIATIONS

PERFECT MANHATTAN
Makes 1 cocktail

2 ounces rye
½ ounce dry vermouth

½ ounce sweet vermouth
Garnish: maraschino cherry

Combine the rye, dry vermouth, and sweet vermouth in a mixing glass with ice and stir until chilled. Strain into a chilled cocktail glass and garnish with the maraschino cherry.

DRY MANHATTAN
Makes 1 cocktail

2 ounces rye
¾ ounce dry vermouth

Garnish: lemon twist

Combine the rye and dry vermouth in a mixing glass with ice and stir until chilled. Strain into a chilled cocktail glass and garnish with the lemon twist.

OLD-FASHIONED

Makes 1 cocktail

The Old-Fashioned is a nod to the original "cocktail" made with sugar, bitters, and water. Although bourbon is considered the canon, you can use any type of spirit. While the traditional recipe requires muddling a sugar cube with the bitters for individual drinks, midcentury hostesses advised using simple syrup when mixing for a crowd.

2 ounces bourbon
½ ounce Simple Syrup
(page 36)

2 dashes aromatic bitters
Garnish: orange peel

Combine the bourbon, simple syrup, and bitters in a mixing glass with ice and stir until well chilled. Strain over a large ice cube into an old-fashioned glass and garnish with the expressed orange peel.

+ FLAVOR INSPIRATION:
For added flavor, crush orange and lemon peels into the sugar, use alternative syrups such as maple or honey, or infuse them with baking spices such as cinnamon, cardamom, or nutmeg.

CLASSIC VARIATION

GIN OLD-FASHIONED

Makes 1 cocktail

2 ounces gin
½ ounce Simple Syrup
(page 36)

2 dashes orange or
grapefruit bitters
Garnish: grapefruit peel

Combine the gin, simple syrup, and bitters in a mixing glass with ice and stir until well chilled. Strain over a large ice cube into an old-fashioned glass and garnish with the expressed grapefruit peel.

HIGHBALL

Makes 1 cocktail

While not strictly a stirred drink, the Highball was often served as a lighter alternative during the midcentury cocktail hour. As Maureen Daly explained in The Perfect Hostess *in 1950, "Highballs are usually served after meals, but some men do seem to like them at cocktail time too."*

2 ounces whiskey	Garnish: lemon slice
Club soda	or twist

Fill an 8- or 10-ounce highball glass with ice, pour in the whiskey, and top with club soda. Garnish with the lemon slice or twist.

CLASSIC VARIATIONS

MOSCOW MULE

Makes 1 cocktail

2 ounces vodka	Garnish: ½ lime, split
Ginger beer	into 2 wedges

Fill a highball glass with ice, pour in the vodka, and fill with the ginger beer. Squeeze the lime wedges over the drink and drop into the cocktail as a garnish.

CUBA LIBRE
Makes 1 cocktail

2 ounces white rum
Cola

Garnish: ½ lime, split into
two wedges

Fill a highball glass with ice, pour in the rum, and fill with the cola. Squeeze the lime wedges over the drink and drop into the cocktail as a garnish.

VII

THE
DINNER PARTY
HOSTESS

c. 1970–1990

*Goodbye to boozing and starving and crowding and screaming,
to five-to-seven and six-to-eight, to the sudden exodus, to the
ruined parlor . . . And welcome, with three loud cheers, to easy
evenings of good wine and good food and good friends.*
—JULIA CHILD, 1979

The cocktail party reached a crescendo of popularity during the 1950s, but from the mid '60s onward began fast falling out of favor; the formal invitation to "Come for cocktails!" replaced with the more casual "Come for drinks!" or simply just "Come to a party!" No longer the chic occasion it had once been, by the late '70s the cocktail party served two main purposes only—either as a small, neighborhood mixer to mark a birthday or holiday, or as a large, formal reception for business networking and publicity purposes.

As social dynamics shifted, the cocktail party gradually became replaced by more informal gatherings, such as the bring-your-own-booze house party and the casual dinner party. For the emerging Dinner Party Hostess, the cocktail was no longer an instrument necessary for her to put on her best show for her guests, but part of a much more personalized ritual expressive of her desire to make those guests feel as relaxed and at home as possible.

So, what happened to the cocktail party as the once universal symbol of home hospitality in America? The answer lies in a social revolution that was changing the way people viewed the culture of hosting, and more important, the role of the hostess within it.

SECOND WAVE FEMINISM
LIBERATES THE HOSTESS

The 1960s were a period of great social change in North America driven by diverse grass-roots movements across gender, sexuality, race, and education that confronted the authority and status quo of the white male ruling class. While much of the radicalization played out on the political stage in the form of the Civil Rights Act and the Equal Pay Act, it also infiltrated popular culture via music, fashion, art, and entertainment.

In 1963, the publication of *The Feminine Mystique*, by Betty Friedan, sparked a feminist revolution that called into question the stereotype of women's identities being defined by their roles in the home. Over the next two decades the rise of second-wave feminism would fight for women's rights in the workplace without discrimination by gender and, by extension, their rights to entertain without reference to their status as wives, housekeepers, and mothers.

One important consequence of this cultural revolution was the widespread rejection of formality and the rigidity of social conventions around gender roles. For the cocktail party, this meant a shift in home hospitality culture from one of fixed times, set drinks, formal dress codes, and hostess service, to one of flexible hours, open bars, come-as-you-are attire, and bring-your-own booze. As women were becoming more liberated, some men also started exploring their own relationships with the home, for once taking a keener interest in historically feminized activities like cooking and entertaining.

As men and women began to take on more blended roles as host and hostess, new styles of party emerged to reflect the change in mood. By the late 1970s and early '80s, cocktail parties were out, and coed house parties and casual dinner parties were in, collectively resulting in the emergence of new cocktail trends.

COME FOR DRINKS!

In 1979, the drinks company Seagram's commissioned the renowned author and beverage expert Sylvia Schur to write a book on drinks and entertaining under the title *Seagram's Complete Party Guide: How to Succeed at Party Planning, Drink Mixing, the Art of Hospitality.* Sylvia was a leading food columnist and editor who had authored more than a dozen books on cooking and regularly covered drinks and entertaining for such popular magazines as *Seventeen, Look,* and *Woman's Home Companion.* A prolific inventor, she also brought several new mixers to the market that are still around today; for instance, Clamato (clam-tomato) juice and Cran-Apple (cranberry-apple) juice.

Seagram's Complete Party Guide reveals the new style of casual drinks party that had taken over from the cocktail party in the late 1970s.

Despite including some 200 cocktail recipes, Sylvia shunned the old formality of drink service for the freedom of an open bar concept that would allow guests to help themselves to any drink they wanted. She recommended this bar be stocked with a full complement of spirits including American whiskey, bourbon, Canadian whisky, gin, scotch, and vodka, plus the options of rum, tequila, and liqueurs, as well as a copious supply of mixers that included club soda, ginger ale or ginger beer, tonic, lemon-lime soda, cola, and their respective diet versions.

With an open bar, Sylvia proposed a "Specialty of Your House Cocktail" for hosts to create an easy signature cocktail for the delight of their guests. The master recipe for this drink consisted of one jigger of liquor, one of a juice or sweet liqueur, shaken or stirred, then either served up, on the rocks, or topped off with a choice of carbonated mixer. For other cocktail options, Sylvia also recommended the prepackaged canned, frozen, and powdered mixes, and ready-to-drink cocktails that were all the rage at the time. For added convenience, these drinks could even be served in plastic cups rather than cocktail glasses, as she wrote, for "quickly made drinks with plus flavor—and plus values."

It seemed that a working knowledge of classic cocktail recipes was no longer a prerequisite for hosting a drinks party anymore. As fellow writer and food influencer Sandra Granseth concurred in her 1981 book *Casual Entertaining*, "If you think bartending requires a degree in mixology, relax, because it doesn't. All you need is an adequate supply of liquor and mixers." By rejecting the strict rules of hosting and drink service that their mothers' generation had obeyed, women of this era liberated themselves from the pressure to be the perfect hostess and were able to focus instead on having a good time alongside their guests. As the rules around the hostess became looser, so too did the rules around the cocktail.

COME FOR DINNER!

Exemplifying the changing rules of hosting, writer, cook, and educator Julia Child, revolutionized the way Americans thought about dining in the second half of the 20th century. Julia had first burst onto the culinary scene in the United States in 1961 with the publication of her seminal book on French cuisine, *Mastering the Art of French Cooking*. A graduate of Le Cordon Bleu school of cooking in Paris, Julia's mission was to bring the joy of traditional French cooking to American households that had become overrun by mass consumerism and manufactured TV dinners. An instant best seller, the book became an award-winning television show, *The French Chef*, and would be followed by nearly 20 more books, a dozen TV series, and multiple Emmy Awards, turning Julia into a national household name.

As her fame continued to grow through the 1970s, Julia not only helped reignite a new appreciation of cooking in America but also, by extension, a new interest in entertaining and the dinner party. However, this dinner party was a far cry from the formal affairs that had taken place in the dark dining rooms or gussied-up parlors of previous generations. Rather, this event took place in the heart of the home—the kitchen. Much like her persona as a television host, as a Dinner Party Hostess, Julia wanted her guests to experience the joy of preparing a meal as much as they did the eating. She dismissed outright the idea that a hostess should toil behind closed kitchen doors while her guests sat awkwardly in the dining room, and instead famously invited her guests to sip on cocktails and chop vegetables at the kitchen table while she prepped and cooked the meal. As she later wrote, "Serious artiste or weekend amateur, it's more fun cooking for company *in* company."

Entertaining in the kitchen also meant that Julia was never far from a bottle of vermouth, and hence the means for a good cocktail. While she was busy at the stove, her husband, Paul, was usually tasked with creating the predinner drink. The couple's signature tipple was said to be a reverse Martini, affectionately dubbed "Ivan's Aperitif" after Julia's brother-in-law, and was made with one jigger each of dry white vermouth, sweet white vermouth, ½ ounce of gin, and an orange twist. Julia included the family's recipe in her 1978 hosting book, *Julia Child & Company*, as well as other signature family cocktails that she mostly credited to Paul. While Paul might have mixed the drinks at home, Julia's charm and national fame propelled his recipes into the public consciousness.

COME FOR WINE!

Through the late 1960s and '70s, many Americans were rejecting what they viewed as the staid social customs of the postwar years and began seeking more exotic epicurean experiences that reflected their increasingly global worldviews. With her reverence for French cuisine and the French culture of dining in general, Julia widely promoted the habit of drinking wine in her books and in her television shows. Indeed, during the decade that *The French Chef* was on air, it is said that America's wine consumption increased by almost 150 percent. In 1981, she cofounded the American Institute of Food and Wine with some well-known US vintners, specifically with the mission to advance the understanding and appreciation of wine and food in the United States.

At the same time, by the late '70s, American wines had started to gain more recognition on the global stage, catalyzing a revolution in both production and consumption that spread from California to Texas to New York. Increasingly, American consumers began replacing spirits with wine at their parties, building cellars in their homes, taking weekend trips to vineyards, and even inventing a new type of elevated drinks party—the wine-tasting party—in honor of their new pastime.

THE QUEEN OF HOSTING

If Julia Child started the dinner party revolution, then it's fair to say that Martha Stewart toppled the ruling power and instated herself as queen. In 1982, her definitive book on hosting, *Entertaining*, catapulted her into fame and turned her into a global media empire. Not since the days of Isabella Beeton would a female host rise to such iconic status that her hosting philosophy would become recognized as a brand in its own right.

Like many other legendary hostesses, Martha had started hosting at a young age. As she wrote in the introduction to *Entertaining*, "When I was in grade school I used to organize all the birthday parties in our neighborhood, just for the fun of arranging little dramas," and she was deep into a flourishing career as an event caterer when she got her break as an author. What Martha observed during her catering years was how the success of an event depended less on whether it followed set rules, and more on whether it had been memorable and meaningful to its guests. Her unique approach to entertaining was to put the personality and style of the host first, which she described as "a totally new style of entertaining that is personal, relaxed, and expressive."

While *Entertaining* was primarily a book of recipes, it was also an ode to the lifestyle of hosting. For, in Martha's world, it was not only what went on the table that mattered, but also how the table was decorated, where in the house it was set, and all the other miscellaneous details that would come together to create an experience that was uniquely special. The book was a revelation, selling over 625,000 copies, and leading to a long-running television series. In the decades that followed, Martha would go on to publish close to 100 more hosting and home management books with topics ranging from cooking to home decor, DIY, crafts, weddings, gardening, and flower arranging.

Although Martha Stewart's career has been famously turbulent at times, it's almost impossible to overstate the level of influence that she has had on the culture of American hosting. In the years since *Entertaining* was first published, her books have sold tens of millions of copies; her best-selling magazine franchise, *Martha Stewart Living*, has reached many millions of subscribers; and her national television series has earned her and her production team back-to-back Emmy Awards. Extending beyond media, Martha's branded homeware collections, lifestyle goods, and wine collaborations have been sold to millions of consumers in retail chains and department stores across the country. And in 1999, she became the first ever female American self-made billionaire when her company, Martha Stewart Living Omnimedia, went public on the New York Stock Exchange.

Martha's emphasis on personality, fresh ingredients, and style coming together in unison in food and home decor extended to the way she also thought about drinks. As she wrote in *Entertaining*, "There is more to serving drinks well than providing appropriate brands in sufficient amounts" and "Drinks will be more interesting and more fun—an entertainment in themselves—if on occasion you add something unexpected to your bar." Her idea was to serve a signature cocktail that reflected both the personality of the host and the theme of the occasion. For example, some of the signature cocktails included in *Entertaining* were the Ocean Sunrise (tequila, cranberry juice, and lime), the Mango Daiquiri (fresh mango, strawberries, and rum), and the Kiwi Cooler (fresh kiwis, coconut cream, and vodka).

Drink recipes would go on to feature heavily in Martha's books, magazines, internet content, and television shows in the years that followed. Still to this day, offering an imaginatively presented "signature" cocktail, as opposed to some standardized bar drink, has become a defining feature of the way Americans host on special occasions.

OPENING THE KITCHEN DOOR

In *Entertaining*, Martha credited Julia Child for inspiring her own career. Julia, she wrote, "for twenty-one years has been my 'companion' in the kitchen," and both women paved the way for scores of female chefs and lifestyle hosts to become global icons in the worlds of food and home entertaining. Highly successful, contemporary television hosts and authors today, such as Ina Garten, Paula Deen, Rachael Ray, Ree Drummond, and Giada De Laurentiis, would surely not be where they are without the trails that Julia and Martha blazed.

Another host whose career once looked set to follow in Martha's footsteps was Barbara "B." Smith who, like Martha, rose to fame as a model, television presenter, lifestyle expert, author, and restaurateur in the late 1980s and early '90s. Her namesake New York City restaurant, B. Smith's, was once described by *Essence* magazine as the place "where the who's who of black Manhattan meet, greet and eat" and she was widely celebrated in the media as "the Black Martha Stewart."

Barbara brought a fresh perspective to American hosting and entertaining through her integration of Black American and global African influences. The B. Smith aesthetic was embodied in her restaurants, hosting books, syndicated television show, and home goods collections that sold in big box stores across the country. Sadly, however, her career was tragically cut short by long-term illness before she was able to reach Martha's level of fame.

DINNER PARTY COCKTAILS

Both Martha Stewart and Julia Child famously liked to entertain in the kitchen because of its more relaxed and intimate atmosphere. As Julia wrote, "We've gotten bored anyway with 'Queen Anne in front and Mary Anne behind': the parlor gussied up with coasters and teeny napkins while frenzy reigns out back."

From the 1960s onward, the great room, which incorporated the kitchen, officially replaced the formal front parlor as the main entertaining space in the American home. Whereas an average parlor might once have accommodated some 20 or 30 standing guests for cocktails, a great room spread out over multiple living areas could easily accommodate 60 or more free-flowing guests. The hostess also had greater flexibility in how she could use this space. For example, she could host a small, intimate group of friends directly from her kitchen island, or use it as a central hub for professional caterers when holding a larger, more formal event.

With guests now congregating in the kitchen, the theme of food and drink became more closely tied. Martha Stewart liked to use fresh ingredients to create her signature drinks, and with rising trends in health and wellness, fruits, herbs, and vegetables became regular features in cocktails during this time. Many popular recipes from this era called for exotic juices, homemade syrups, and the blending of whole fruits directly into drinks. Garnishes, also, were no longer just a simple twist or citrus slice, but entire skewers of fruit balanced over the drink along-side other elaborately crafted decorations. Through the early 2000s, woman-authored cocktail books popularized fruit-based drinks, such as blender drinks, pitcher drinks, tropical drinks, summer drinks, and even alcohol-laced smoothies. Example titles included *Summer Cocktails*, by Penelope Wisner; *Tipsy Smoothies*, by Donna Pliner Rodnitzky; *101 Great Tropical Drinks*, by Cheryl Chee Tsutsumi; and *Frozen Drinks*, by Cheryl Charming.

At this time, the blender took over from the cocktail shaker as the most common tool in the mixologist's kitchen. Blenders were already a common household appliance in the 1950s, but really came into their own as frozen cocktails got more popular over the coming decades. The loud, mechanical whir of blades in a blender replacing the soft clatter of ice in a shaker as the signal to guests that the party had begun. One consequence of this trend was that certain cocktails that had previously been popular as shaken drinks, such as the Daiquiri or Margarita, were now more likely to be consumed in their frozen or blended forms with other fruits, juices, and liqueurs added in. As everyone learned how to mix a Margarita at home, tequila also grew in popularity.

However, the spirit that grew exponentially during this time was vodka. Vodka had been popular since the 1950s, but by the '80s had overtaken whiskey as the number one spirit in the United States. Vodka's appeal lay in its "clean" image—a colorless, flavorless, odorless liquor that could provide the buzz to a prepackaged mixer, juice, or soft drink; would not overpower the flavor of a fruit-based cocktail; and was also widely believed at the time to result in less of a hangover the next day.

FRUIT COCKTAILS

SCREWDRIVER

Makes 1 cocktail

Vodka with a juice mixer featured on most house party menus during the 1970s and '80s. The Screwdriver is one of the most reminiscent of these fruit cocktails and can be found alongside many similar variations, like the Salty Dog and Tequila Sunrise, in such books as Sylvia Schur's 1979 Seagram's Complete Party Guide.

1½ ounces vodka	**Fresh orange juice**

Add ice to a double old-fashioned glass or highball glass. Pour in the vodka and top with the orange juice. The drink does not traditionally call for a garnish.

 ✦ *FLAVOR INSPIRATION:*
Adding a liqueur to the Screwdriver recipe makes well-known variations, such as the Slow Screw (with sloe gin), the Fuzzy Navel (with peach schnapps), and the Harvey Wallbanger (with Galliano liqueur).

CLASSIC VARIATIONS

SALTY DOG
Makes 1 cocktail

1½ ounces vodka
Fresh grapefruit juice

Coarse salt (optional)

Add ice to a highball glass. Pour in the vodka and fill with the grapefruit juice. Sprinkle coarse salt over the top of the drink. When made with gin instead of vodka, this cocktail is known as a Greyhound.

TEQUILA SUNRISE
Makes 1 cocktail

1½ ounces tequila
Fresh orange juice

1 teaspoon grenadine
or Raspberry Syrup
(page 37)

Add ice to a highball glass. Pour the tequila and grenadine over the ice, then fill with orange juice. When made with grapefruit juice instead of orange juice, this cocktail is known as a Tequila Sunstroke.

BLOODY MARY

Makes 1 cocktail

Popular at brunch since the midcentury, the Bloody Mary is the exemplification of the appetizer-meets-cocktail beverage trend that took over during the Dinner Party Hostess's era. Martha Stewart was an early promoter of the Bloody Mary bar concept, a fun way for guests to season and personalize their own drinks using additional condiments and garnishes offered on the side.

1½ ounces vodka
½ ounce fresh lemon juice
4 ounces tomato juice
Dash of Worcestershire
    sauce

Dash of hot pepper sauce
Pinch of celery salt
Pinch of freshly ground
    black pepper
Garnish: celery stick

Combine all the ingredients, except the celery stick, in a cocktail shaker with ice and lightly rock side to side (rather than shake) to blend and chill. Strain into a highball glass filled with more ice, and garnish with the celery stick.

✦ *FLAVOR INSPIRATION:*

Optional additional seasonings to add to a Bloody Mary bar include horseradish sauce, fresh garlic, balsamic vinegar, and alternative hot pepper sauces. Garnish choices include sticks of cucumber, olives, pickles, citrus slices, and skewers of cooked bacon or shrimp. Using Sylvia Schur's choice of Clamato juice makes a variation called a Bloody Caesar, whereas a mix of orange and tomato juice makes a Bloody Sunrise; and tomato juice with beer, a Bloody Brew.

CLASSIC VARIATIONS

BLOODY MARIA
Makes 1 cocktail

1½ ounces tequila
½ ounce fresh lime juice
4 ounces tomato juice
Dash of Worcestershire
  sauce

Dash of hot pepper sauce
Pinch of celery salt
Pinch of freshly ground
  black pepper
Garnish: celery stick

Combine all the ingredients, except the celery stick, in a cocktail shaker with ice and lightly rock side to side (rather than shake) to blend and chill. Strain into a highball glass filled with more ice and garnish with the celery stick.

RED SNAPPER
Makes 1 cocktail

1½ ounces gin
½ ounce fresh lemon juice
4 ounces tomato juice
Dash of Worcestershire
  sauce

Dash of hot pepper sauce
Pinch of celery salt
Pinch of freshly ground
  black pepper
Garnish: celery stick

Combine all the ingredients, except the celery stick, in a cocktail shaker with ice and lightly rock side to side (rather than shake) to blend and chill. Strain into a highball glass filled with more ice and garnish with the celery stick.

FROZEN DAIQUIRI

Makes 1 cocktail

Long before the Margarita, the Daiquiri was a classic sour cocktail that had been around since the turn of the 20th century, but reached even greater heights of fame when it found its way into the blenders of the home host from the midcentury onward. The recipe for the first ever Frozen Strawberry Daiquiri is said to have appeared in Mabel Stegner's book Electric Blender Recipes, *published in 1952.*

2 ounces light rum
1 ounce fresh lime juice

1 ounce Simple Syrup
(page 36)

Combine all the ingredients in a blender with ½ cup of ice and blend until the drink has a smooth, even consistency. Serve in a large coupe or hurricane glass.

+ *FLAVOR INSPIRATION:*

By infusing the rum base with fruit, changing out the simple syrup for a fruit-flavored syrup or liqueur, or by adding fresh fruit directly to the mix, a whole new world of flavor options is at your fingertips.

CLASSIC VARIATIONS

STRAWBERRY DAIQUIRI
Makes 1 cocktail

2 ounces light rum
½ ounce fresh lime juice

1 ounce Strawberry Syrup
(see Raspberry Syrup,
page 37) or liqueur
Garnish: fresh strawberry

Combine all the ingredients in a blender with ½ cup of ice and blend until the drink has a smooth, even consistency. Serve in a large coupe or hurricane glass, garnished with the strawberry.

FROZEN MARGARITA
Makes 1 cocktail

2 ounces tequila
¾ ounce Triple Sec (page 43)
1 ounce lime juice

¼ ounce Simple Syrup
(page 36)

Combine all the ingredients in a blender with half a cup of ice and blend until the drink has a smooth, even consistency. Serve in a large coupe or hurricane glass.

PIÑA COLADA

Makes 1 cocktail

The Piña Colada is the ultimate tropical vacation drink and is single-handedly responsible for giving cream of coconut a permanent place in the cocktail pantry. Alongside the Frozen Daiquiri, it was the symbol of the blender drink movement during the 1970s and '80s. Still to this day, it's worth keeping cans of coconut, pineapple juice, and miniature paper umbrellas on hand for whenever the urge to escape to the beach takes hold.

2 ounces light rum
1½ ounces cream of coconut
1½ ounces pineapple juice

½ ounce fresh lime juice
Garnish: pineapple
slice or spear

Combine the rum, cream of coconut, pineapple juice, and lime juice in a blender with ½ cup of crushed ice and blend on low speed until the drink has a smooth, even consistency. Serve in a hurricane glass, tiki mug, or collins glass. Can also be served shaken and poured over crushed ice. Garnish with the pineapple slice or spear.

+ *FLAVOR INSPIRATION:*

Change out the pineapple juice for a flavored syrup or liqueur, or blend in some fresh fruit, such as banana, mango, passion fruit, guava or strawberry. A Piña Colada and Strawberry Daiquiri swirled together makes the decadent summertime treat known as a Miami Vice.

CLASSIC VARIATION

PAINKILLER
Makes 1 cocktail

2 ounces dark rum

4 ounces pineapple juice

1 ounce fresh orange juice

1 ounce cream of coconut

Freshly grated nutmeg

Combine the rum, pineapple juice, orange juice, and cream of coconut in a cocktail shaker with ice and shake until chilled. Strain into a tiki mug or highball glass that has been filled with crushed or cobbled ice, then grate the nutmeg over the top of the drink.

VIII

THE
CITY HOSTESS

c. 1990–2010

*For our generation, socializing in bars is second nature,
and in spite of the fact that men originally dominated
watering holes, the girls are just as good at it as the boys.
Though guys never did seem to mind the invasion.*
—NICOLE BELAND, 2003

I f second-wave feminism unshackled the Suburban Hostess from the rigid social norms of entertaining in the midcentury, then third wave feminism of the 1990s paved the way for the arrival of an even more liberated cocktail-drinking woman, the City Hostess. The most striking characteristic of the City Hostess that set her apart from previous generations was that she was no longer just hosting at home anymore; this hostess was now taking over bars and restaurants, and entertaining people however and wherever she pleased. And once again, her changing behavior set off even more new trends in the world of the cocktail that still resonate today.

To understand where the City Hostess came from, we first need to go back to a parallel trend in social behavior that was happening right around the time that the Dinner Party Hostess was also getting her start.

THE PARLOR COMES TO THE BAR

One lasting consequence of the norms of home entertaining in midcentury North America was that men and women were drinking regularly at home together and, by the Dinner Party Hostess era, coed hosted drinks parties had become standard protocol in most homes. However, at the start of the 1960s, despite men and women enjoying cocktails together at their house parties, still very few bars were actually open to, or friendly to, female patrons who were unaccompanied by some kind of male chaperone.

As explored in the previous chapter, however, this began to change during the 1960s and '70s as women started fighting for their right to take up space both inside and outside the house, leading hostesses to reject their role as home waitress and server. And with changing social attitudes toward women's roles also came their quest for sexual adventure. With the widespread availability of the contraceptive pill women no longer sought men's permission to explore a life outside of marriage, home, and the family. Now, all that this newly liberated female drinker needed was a place to meet up with a few like-minded friends. Enter: the fern bar.

During the '60s and '70s, enterprising bar owners in US coastal cities, such as New York and San Francisco, realized it might be good for business if they could actually attract more women into their establishments, and that in so doing, the tone of their bars might improve overall. Fern bars were so called because of the kitsch way they mimicked the home parlor environment by using interior decorations like vintage lamps, potted plants, and brightly colored wallpapers, with the express purpose of attracting and welcoming a more female crowd.

The premise of the fern bar was that if female customers were happy, male customers would be too since the prospect of meeting more women would keep them drinking in the bar for longer. As such, fern bars became ideal places for single men and women to meet and mingle. This was facilitated not only by the decor, but also through the food and drink menus. Cheap shareable appetizer plates, such as Buffalo wings, nachos, and loaded potato skins became all the rage at fern bars, as did fruit- and liqueur-based cocktails like the Fuzzy Navel and Lemon Drop, mixed specifically to appeal to women's preferences.

The fern bar concept took off in a big way during the 1970s and early '80s, spreading to pretty much every town in America. Several national restaurant franchises, such as TGI Fridays, Bennigan's, and Houlihan's, capitalized on the trend, establishing themselves as the go-to places for young men and women to hang out. Unfortunately, the tackiness of the phenomenon made it a relatively short-lived trend. However, the culture of ladies' nights and singles bars grew ever stronger, and by the time the 1990s rolled around, women's tastes had become established as one of the main drivers of drink offerings in bars wherever a romantic encounter might be on the menu.

SEX AND THE COCKTAIL

Of course, the relationship between sex and the cocktail has always been there, lurking under the surface of a freshly poured drink and ready to pounce the moment spirits are high and inhibitions are low. In the 1920s, when men and women were sharing their bibulous libations at clandestine apartment parties, cocktails with cheeky monikers like Between the Sheets, Bosom Caresser, and Hanky Panky were all the rage. Then, after the regressive sexual conservatism of the 1950s, the tawdriness of the cocktail rose to a whole new level with the arrival of the swinging sixties. In the 1960s and '70s, it became literal sport to sidle up to a bar and shout for a Slow Screw, Sex on the Beach, or Harvey Wallbanger while giving a nod and a wink to any available singles who might be within earshot.

In the 1980s and '90s, all inhibitions and any pretense at cocktail sophistication pretty much fell by the wayside when shooters joined the party. Essentially mini-cocktails in shot form, short drinks with sexually charged names like the Slippery Nipple, Blow Job, and Screaming Orgasm would be lined up in suggestively shaped glasses on the tops of bars and slurped off the half-naked body parts of alcohol-soaked revelers.

It is probably fair to say that the sexual and social emancipation of women has been a key driver in their exploration of the cocktail throughout the second half of the 20th century. In 1962, one year before Betty Friedan's *The Feminine Mystique* came out, Helen Gurley Brown published an alternative feminist manifesto called *Sex and the Single Girl: The Unmarried Woman's Guide to Men, Careers, the Apartment, Diet, Fashion, Money and Men*. Some 30 years since Marjorie Hillis had once advised women that living a single life might be possible, even desirable, Helen was now showing a whole new generation of girls that a sexually and financially liberated life was in many ways the holy grail.

Sex and the Single Girl was a breakaway success. The book reportedly sold two million copies in its first three weeks of publication and went on to be released in over two dozen countries, remaining on the best seller lists for over a year. Helen herself became an instant icon and role model for women seeking sexual freedom and social independence. In 1965, she was recruited to take over as editor in chief of *Cosmopolitan* magazine, and over the next 30 years, she would go on to revolutionize women's media and turn *Cosmopolitan* into one of the most widely read women's magazines in the world.

The Helen Gurley Brown philosophy, which ultimately became the *Cosmopolitan* philosophy, was that women could, and *should*, have it all—be it love, sex, glamour, fashion, or money. This doctrine eventually found its peak in the third-wave feminism movement of the 1990s, when women who had established their workplace and marriage rights, now began reclaiming their rights to their own femininity and to express this through such traditionally male pursuits as material success, sexual accomplishment, and drinks.

Third-wave feminism had several consequences for the cocktail drinking City Hostess. First of all, she lost any remaining reticence about entering bars unescorted by men and began hosting her friends in bars, and if she wanted to, even drinking by herself. Second, now that she was able to pursue her own financial gain, she had the disposable income to use on herself, which included big spends on things like designer clothes, five-star meals, and high-end jewelry, as well as on more day-to-day luxuries like cocktails. And third, she had the confidence to start exploring her own tastes in drinks by ordering cocktails exactly the way she wanted them. This resulted in an explosion in woman-driven cocktail trends that dominated menus in restaurants and bars around the world for close to a decade.

COSMO GIRLS CAUSE A STIR

During the 1990s, the word *cosmopolitan* became cultural code for women seeking sexual adventure; however, it also became drink code for the Cosmo Girl's signature cocktail, the Cosmopolitan.

The Cosmopolitan cocktail is believed to have first appeared in the gay bar scene of San Francisco in the 1970s but exploded more or less everywhere in the late 1980s and early '90s. The story goes that the drink first came to New York City in the late '80s when two female customers from San Francisco requested it at the Odeon, an ultrahip restaurant in Manhattan. The head bartender of the Odeon began playing around with the recipe and the drink quickly became a staff favorite. Soon, the it-girl and celebrity clientele of the bar started ordering them, and it was not long before it spread to other New York City establishments, too. The cocktail gained national attention in 1996 when the pop icon Madonna was photographed sipping one at a Grammys afterparty at the Rainbow Room. Then, a few years later, it would go stratospheric when the characters of the hit HBO television series *Sex and the City* were portrayed drinking Cosmopolitans, instantly turning it into the signature cocktail of the show's many million fans.

Around this time, the journalist Nicole Beland was commissioned to write a drinking guide for the new cocktail-loving woman, titled *The Cocktail Jungle: A Girl's Field Guide to Shaking and Stirring*. A senior editor in her twenties at—you guessed it—*Cosmopolitan* magazine, Nicole detailed everything the modern hostess should know about the urban cocktail scene. This included what types of bars to visit, typical drinks on the menu, the typology of men to be found there, and how to attract them. In keeping with the magazine's ethos, the guide also included lifestyle features, such as a cocktail astrology guide, interviews with leading female bartenders, the favorite drinks of female icons like Madonna and Coco Chanel, and party tips for the hostess who wanted to re-create her bar experiences at home.

Among the 50 or so cocktail recipes in the book were variations of many popular drinks of the time, including the Cosmopolitan, naturally, as well as such drinks as Mojitos, Margaritas, Martinis, and even some classic cocktails. To research the book, Nicole interviewed bartenders from some of the hippest bars in the country, traveling from New York City to New Orleans to Los Angeles.

Published in 2003, *The Cocktail Jungle* is arguably the most colorful representation of the City Hostess and her cocktail drinking habits of this era. The book was given a glamorous launch party in New York City, written up in the *New York Times*, and retailed in hip fashion stores, such as Urban Outfitters. After the success of the book, Nicole herself went on to become executive editor of *Cosmopolitan* magazine and to publish three more books on sex and relationships for the forward-thinking metropolitan woman.

Such was the commercial power of the City Hostess that several other books written by women, for women, also came out around this time. These included such titles as *Highballs High Heels: A Girl's Guide to the Art of Cocktails*, by Karen Brooks and others; *The Pink Drink Book*, by Jaclyn Foley; *Sexy City Cocktails*, by Sheree Bykofsky and Megan Buckley; and *Flirtini: A Guide to Mixing and Mingling*, by Allana Baroni.

THE MARTINI IS REBORN

Prior to the 1990s, the original dry Martini had always had a reputation as a bit of a man's drink. It had been the favorite tipple of several former presidents and, as Nicole Beland wrote, was often portrayed in popular culture as "the signature drink of the successful—and slightly stressed—executive." This image was further reinforced by the iconography of its glass—the masculine austerity of its sharp angles giving the aura of a drinker who was urbane and upscale, yet at the same time somewhat aloof and uptight.

However, the arrival of the Cosmopolitan changed the image of the Martini, and its glass, almost overnight. For when this same glass was filled with the glistening elixir of the Cosmopolitan, it was instantly transformed into an unquestionably female totem. The broad sides encasing a bright pink interior and tapering to a gently rounded apex atop a long, slender stem now bore more than a passing resemblance to that certain part of a woman's anatomy. It can be no coincidence that the popularity of the Cosmopolitan reached its crescendo right when *Sex and the City* was being aired on television and *The Vagina Monologues* was being performed on stage. Just putting the Cosmopolitan to one's lips was, to all intents and purposes, an homage to female sexual pleasure.

During the late '90s and early aughts, as women began to claim certain cocktails like the Cosmopolitan as their own, they also began using cocktails as a way to explore their identity. As Nicole Beland wrote, "We're trying them on like clothes and keeping them only if we like them." This adventuresome attitude had an impact on the cocktail by loosening boundaries between different cocktail genres and expanding categories to include new forms and flavors.

Nowhere was this more prevalent than in the Martini. Well beyond the Cosmopolitan, in the '90s the Martini went through a complete transformation. Essentially, now any drink with vodka, mixed with some other flavored aperitif or liqueur and served up in a martini glass, could be categorized as a Martini. Indeed, just as the martini glass became the universally recognized symbol of the cocktail, "'tini" became established in the cocktail lexicon as a suffix that was attachable to almost any drink moniker, Martini or not.

In the late '90s, a number of highly successful books were published on the Martini, including several by women. For example, *The Martini Book*, by Sally Ann Berk, explored the many 'tini variations of the drink and became the subject of numerous tasting blogs among its devoted female followers. Meanwhile, *Shaken Not Stirred: A Celebration of the Martini*, by cocktail enthusiasts Anistatia Miller and Jared Brown, explored the evolution and history of the drink. The book, which had originally started out as a blog, reportedly sold over half a million copies and was the launchpad for the authors' successful careers as cocktail writers, researchers, and global industry experts.

SKINNY IS THE NEW 'TINI

In 2008, a few years after Carrie Bradshaw and her friends were ordering Cosmopolitans in the fictional *Sex and the City* series, entrepreneur and Manhattan socialite Bethenny Frankel was filmed ordering what she called a "skinny girl's Margarita" on the hit Bravo reality television series *The Real Housewives of New York City*. The drink consisted of tequila, lime juice, and "a little splash of triple sec," and it started one of the fastest growing cocktail trends of the early aughts, simultaneously turning Bethenny into a multimillionaire.

A year after she first ordered a skinny Margarita on national television, Bethenny had the idea to build a business around the drink and the Skinnygirl lifestyle more generally. In 2009, she published her diet manifesto, titled *Naturally Thin: Unleash Your Skinnygirl*, and launched the ready-to-drink cocktail brand Skinnygirl Margarita, promoting it to *Real Housewives'* many million viewers. The business quickly took off and expanded to become the cocktail and consumer goods company Skinnygirl. Within two years, the global drinks giant Beam Suntory had acquired Bethenny's cocktail business for reportedly over $100 million, and expanded the range to include flavored vodkas, ready-to-drink cocktails, and wines.

By tapping into women's collective body consciousness, Bethenny quickly found a connection with a large segment of women drinkers whose desires and concerns were being overlooked by the big liquor brands at that time. As she later wrote, "I love a cocktail. But what I don't love is that the usual drinks are packed with needless calories . . . I wanted to have a signature cocktail that I could drink when I was out and wouldn't leave me feeling bloated and hungover the next day."

A few years later, Bethenny published her own cocktail guide, *Skinnygirl Cocktails*, and in the book described her formula for the archetypal low-calorie cocktail, which she dubbed the "Skinnygirl Fixologist Formula." The recipe consisted of one shot of clear liquor, such as vodka or tequila, a splash of a fruit juice or liqueur, club soda, and a fruit garnish. Whether it was Bethenny's invention or not, the something-and-soda-with-a-splash cocktail became one of the most called for drinks in America in the late aughts and remains a familiar order in bars to this day.

CITY COCKTAILS

With City Hostesses now taking up equal space in bars, it was inevitable that they would start to bring their experiences back home as well. As

Karen Brooks and her coauthors wrote in their 2001 *Highballs High Heels*, "Girls have always outscored their male competitors on the social index" and "Let's face it: girls have the upper hand in the get-together universe." With a renewed fascination for cocktails came a reawakening of interest in the cocktail party, with books like Leslie Brenner's *The Art of the Cocktail Party* and Martha Gill's *Modern Cocktails and Appetizers* calling for a revival of this retro way of entertaining. While formal "cocktail parties," in their strictest sense, continued to be held as mostly publicity events, house parties fueled by cocktails surged in popularity again during the early aughts.

As the Apartment Hostess had done nearly a century before, the City Hostess used her apartment as the main venue for the new cocktail party. However, rather than as an alternative to the bar scene, this time cocktails were a way for her to show off her knowledge of the latest bar trends and bring the ambience of the bar back to her own cocktail parlor. For example, if she wanted to throw an after-hours karaoke session, she might serve up Lychee Martinis and sake-based cocktails to her crooning guests. While if she preferred to let loose in a south of the border–style birthday fiesta, she might go for a Margarita bar setup instead. The cocktails also inspired her choice of party music, decor, and accessories. With a quick trip to the local party store, her apartment could be transformed into a tiki bar, a karaoke club, or a jazz lounge with just a sprinkling of a few appropriately printed cocktail napkins, some strategically placed tea lights, and all manner of other cheaply available decorative party knickknacks.

Aside from the Margarita, which was by now ranked as the top cocktail in America, vodka was very much king of the spirits during this era, and the Martini/'tini the drink order of the day. It was a simple formula. An ounce or two of plain or flavored vodka, some flavor-giving element like a liqueur, an occasional splash of juice, and a playfully matching garnish. As Sally Ann Berk wrote in *The Martini Book*, "The modern martini mixer makes use of the flavored vodkas. Everything from coffee-flavored to pepper-flavored is on the shelves of your liquor store." As for the garnish, the more creative the better. Per Sally, "There is no limit to what you can use as a garnish . . . if you think it's a garnish, then it is." Unsurprisingly then, vodka drinks and 'tinis ruled the home menus of the City Hostess.

However, it should also be noted that, oftentimes, the drinks from this period have been treated with derision, labelled as "girly drinks," and generally looked down upon by some (usually male) drinkers and certain sections of the mixology elite. Yet this critique belies the truth, which is that at the time, literally *everyone* was drinking them. As Nicole Beland bore witness in *The Cocktail Jungle*, "[Guys have] started to follow our lead and are finally ordering all the sweet, colorful concoctions we've been raving about for years. A Stud holding a Sour-Apple Martini is no longer a rare sight." Even today, these drinks continue to be enjoyed by anyone who appreciates simple, flavorful, fun cocktails.

'TINI COCKTAILS

COSMOPOLITAN

Makes 1 cocktail

Much like its drinker, the Cosmopolitan of the 1990s was colorful, feminine, decadent, and just the right amount of sassy. The cocktail has fallen in and out of favor many times over the years, yet remains one of those drinks that people love-to-hate and love-to-drink in equal measure.

2 ounces vodka
1 ounce Triple Sec
   (page 43)
1 ounce cranberry juice

½ ounce fresh lime juice
Garnish: citrus
   twist (optional)

Combine all the ingredients, except the citrus twist, in a cocktail shaker with ice and shake until well chilled. Strain into a martini glass or coupe. Garnish, if desired, with a citrus twist.

+ *FLAVOR INSPIRATION:*
Try an infused vodka such as lemon, orange, or cherry as the base, or use white cranberry juice instead of the usual red for a variation called the White Cosmopolitan.

CLASSIC SHOOTERS

KAMIKAZE
Makes 1 cocktail

1 ounce vodka

½ ounce Triple Sec (page 43)

½ ounce fresh lime juice

Combine the ingredients in a cocktail shaker with ice and shake until well chilled. Strain into a shooter glass.

WOO WOO
Makes 1 cocktail

½ ounce vodka

½ ounce peach schnapps

½ ounce cranberry juice

Combine the ingredients in a cocktail shaker with ice and shake until well chilled. Strain into a shooter glass.

LEMON DROP MARTINI

Makes 1 cocktail

The invention of the Lemon Drop dates back to the fern bar craze of the 1970s and went through a second wave of popularity in the '90s. As Karen Brooks recalled in the 2001 Highballs High Heels, *"It started with a lemonade stand on the sidewalk next to your parents' driveway. . . . That sweet, light, always-on-the-edge flavor of youth has grown up and become a force of cocktail culture."*

2 ounces lemon vodka
¼ ounce Triple Sec (page 43)
¾ ounce fresh lemon juice

½ ounce Simple Syrup
(page 36)
Garnish: lemon twist

Combine all the ingredients, except the lemon twist, in a cocktail shaker with ice and shake until well chilled. Strain into a martini glass or coupe. Garnish with the lemon twist.

✦ *FLAVOR INSPIRATION:*
Replace the simple syrup with Raspberry Syrup (page 37) to make a fruity Pink Lemon Drop.

CLASSIC SHOOTER

LEMON DROP SHOOTER

Makes 1 cocktail

½ ounce lemon vodka
½ ounce Triple Sec (page 43)

½ ounce fresh lemon juice

Cmbine all the ingredients in a cocktail shaker with ice and shake until well chilled. Strain into shooter glass.

APPLETINI

Makes 1 cocktail

The Appletini may have started out as a fad, but it became the archetype for the whole category of 'tinis in the 1990s. In The Cocktail Jungle, *Nicole Beland defines the genre as "fashionable libations [that] hold loads of liquor but are still very feminine." When drinking an Appletini, she continued, "onlookers will peg you as a fun party girl who likes to pamper herself. Guys will be equal parts intimidated and fascinated."*

---

2 ounces vodka
1 ounce sour apple liqueur

Garnish: apple slice soaked in lemon juice

Combine the vodka and sour apple liqueur in a cocktail shaker with ice and shake until well chilled. Strain into a chilled martini glass or coupe. Garnish with the apple slice.

+ *FLAVOR INSPIRATION:*
  A sugar rim adds a sweet touch to this cocktail. An ounce or two of apple cider can be added to lengthen the drink.

CLASSIC VARIATIONS

LYCHEE MARTINI
Makes 1 cocktail

2 ounces vodka
1 ounce lychee liqueur

Garnish: whole
peeled lychee

Combine the vodka and lychee liqueur in a cocktail shaker with ice and shake until well chilled. Strain into a chilled martini glass or coupe. Garnish with the lychee.

GINGER MARTINI
Makes 1 cocktail

2 ounces vodka
1 ounce ginger liqueur

Garnish: piece of
candied ginger

Combine the vodka and ginger liqueur in a cocktail shaker with ice and shake until well chilled. Strain into a chilled martini glass or coupe. Garnish with the candied ginger.

ESPRESSO MARTINI

Makes 1 cocktail

According to legend, the first Espresso Martini was mixed in London in the 1980s, when an unnamed supermodel asked a bartender to make her a drink that would "f*** me up and then wake me up." Many cocktail enthusiasts have since tried and failed to track down this feisty diva who inadvertently started one of the biggest boomerang cocktail crazes of the last 30 years.

1 ounce vodka	1 ounce coffee liqueur
1 ounce hot brewed espresso	Garnish: 3 coffee beans

To ensure the crema of the coffee is preserved, use hot espresso. Combine the vodka, espresso, and coffee liqueur in a cocktail shaker with lots of ice and shake hard until chilled. Strain into a chilled cocktail glass. Garnish with the coffee beans.

+ *FLAVOR INSPIRATION:*

Some like to express a lemon peel over the finished drink. If the coffee is especially bitter, add a small amount of Simple Syrup (page 36) to taste. Replacing the vodka with cognac makes the luxurious Cognac Espresso Martini.

BLACK RUSSIAN
Makes 1 cocktail

2 ounces vodka   Cola (optional)
¾ ounce coffee liqueur

Combine the vodka and coffee liqueur in a mixing glass with ice and stir to chill. Strain over fresh ice into a double old-fashioned glass. Add one to two splashes of cola (if using).

WHITE RUSSIAN
Makes 1 cocktail

2 ounces vodka   Heavy cream
¾ ounce coffee liqueur

Combine the vodka and coffee liqueur in a mixing glass with ice and stir to chill. Strain over fresh ice into a double old-fashioned glass. Add one to two splashes of heavy cream.

IX

THE CRAFT
HOSTESS

c. 2000–2020

*I think women make wonderful bartenders because we like to take
care of people. We're more attentive to others' needs.*
—AUDREY SAUNDERS, 2003

During the City Hostess's era, women were already asserting themselves as customers in front of the bar, but in the Craft Hostess's era they began dominating behind the bar as well. As the collective interest in fruit drinks, frozen drinks, and 'tini drinks began to fade, women rose to the forefront of the craft cocktail revival. Not only did women become some of the most influential bar owners and mixologists during this time, rediscovering old classic cocktails and inventing new ones, but as writers and researchers, they also drove the dissemination of cocktail culture to an ever wider audience.

In the early 21st century, Craft Hostesses have challenged the norms of the cocktail and the female drinker, and in particular the stereotype of women only enjoying sweet or fruity cocktails. As bitter drinks have risen in popularity, certain cocktails and spirits that were once considered off limits for women have become the center of a new movement around flavor. And as Craft Hostesses have professionalized the art of the cocktail, they have combined their drinks intelligence with centuries of hosting wisdom to catalyze a whole new cocktail movement.

A BRIEF HISTORY OF WOMEN BEHIND THE BAR

Up until the mid-1800s, women had been able to pursue decent careers and social status as tavern keepers and barmaids in the United States, until the end of the first industrial revolution, when the Victorians created social and legal structures that separated the sexes. As saloon culture took over in the 19th century, many states went as far as to outlaw the presence of women in bars. In states where women were permitted as patrons, they frequently had to enter through a side entrance. And in those states where women could be employed in a bar, it was often either solely as a waitress or as the wife or daughter of the owner.

However, as we have seen, the culture of women in bars began to shift dramatically with Prohibition as women frequented underground speakeasies and served cocktails at their home parties. During the Second World War, the number of women bartenders spiked when a male labor shortage led many waitresses to take up positions behind the bar. Yet, after the men returned home from war, they overturned this social progress by demanding their jobs back. Although their motives may have been partly economic in nature, they were also outspoken in their paternalistic view that women were less suited to the physicality of bartending and/or that the work was simply unbecoming to a woman.

As a result, hotel and restaurant unions across the country passed resolutions reclaiming the profession of bartending for men, and in the years that followed, more than half the states in the United States retained some form of legislation prohibiting women from working in bars. In 1940, only 3 percent of the bartending population was said to be female, and in 1948, a challenge to the state law in Michigan brought about by a widowed bar owner, Valentine Goesaert, and her daughter, Margaret, even made it all the way to the United States Supreme Court, where the case was promptly shot down.

However, with the equal rights movement of the 1960s and '70s, legislation and contract restrictions on women working in a variety of fields began to ease and the numbers of female bartenders steadily rose from around 1 in 5 in the early '70s to more than half in the '90s. Today, women, in fact, represent the majority of bartenders in the United States. However, the public perception of the profession and its representation in popular culture—indeed, even *within* the trade itself—continues to be that it is a predominantly male occupation.

THE CRAFT COCKTAIL RENAISSANCE

During the 1990s, while most home hosts and mainstream bartenders were busy mixing their pitchers of frozen margaritas and neon Appletinis, a handful of mixologists were rediscovering the bartending manuals of a century before and revitalizing the old craft of mixology. One of the central hubs in the early days of the revival was the Rainbow Room in

New York City, which was presided over by legendary bartender Dale DeGroff. When Dale was not serving Cosmopolitans to the likes of Madonna at Grammys after-parties, he was re-creating and perfecting the drinks of yesteryear, many of which had not been served in bars for several generations. He was also educating a new school of bartenders who would go on to have glittering careers at the forefront of the cocktail revival. Two of the most influential figures to emerge from this school were Audrey Saunders and Julie Reiner.

In 2003, Audrey had been hired by Dale to manage a classic cocktail program at the legendary Bemelmans Bar at the Carlyle Hotel in New York City, when she was interviewed by Nicole Beland for her book *The Cocktail Jungle*. Audrey contributed several recipes to the book, including a Whiskey Smash and a rum and Champagne drink she would later become famous for, called the Old Cuban. She also spoke to Nicole about the important role women had to play as professional bartenders due to their unique skill sets, diverse palates, and passion for service. As she shared about her own experiences behind the bar, "I'll say hello to someone who walks into the bar and try to sense what kind of a day they're having. And I really do want to make them the perfect cocktail—the one that's going to turn their day around, perk them up, and make them feel like a fun night has started."

Audrey's passion for the craft of bartending turned her into one of the most influential professionals of the recent era. In 2005, after leaving Bemelmans, she would go on to launch and operate Pegu Club in Manhattan, which in 15 years it was open, was considered one of the leading cocktail bars in the world.

One of Audrey's business partners at Pegu was Julie Reiner, another bartending legend and proprietor of the award-winning New York City bars Flatiron Lounge and Clover Club. Over the years, Julie has been widely recognized by the bartending industry for her strong commercial acumen, sophisticated palate, and innovative use of culinary ingredients in drinks. In addition, she has been a longtime champion of women in the industry, demonstrating in her own bars that when women are behind the stick the service tends to be more attentive, the cocktail menus more creative, and the patrons better behaved.

Julie's influence on modern mixology extends well beyond the trade, however. A regular commentator in high-end media, such as the *New York Times* and *Bon Appétit*, she has also appeared on mainstream television to talk about cocktails, including on the *Today* show and the Food Network. In 2015, she collaborated with Kaitlyn Goalen to put some of her best recipes to paper in *The Craft Cocktail Party*. In their book, Julie shares her professional perspective on the principles of cocktail making and recalls the story of how she first learned the skill of hospitality from watching her parents host cocktail parties. Dedicating the book to her mother, she wrote, "I now realize that I was a host long before I tasted my first cocktail" and "I didn't know it then, but that act of welcoming someone into one's home with a glass of something refreshing and delicious made a permanent impression on me."

As the craft cocktail revival went mainstream in the late 2000s, it reignited the whole profession of bartending, with several individuals reaching heights of celebrity previously reserved only for the top chefs. With this newfound fame came multiple book deals; and many women, like Julie, were able to break through the proverbial tin ceiling with specialist cocktail books that have featured continuously on best cocktail book lists. Such women and their works as Shannon Mustipher's *Modern Tropical Cocktails*, Ivy Mix's *Spirits of Latin America*, Julia Momosé's *The Way of the Cocktail: Japanese Traditions, Techniques, and Recipes*, Natasha David's *Drink Lightly*, and Alba Huerta's *Julep: Southern Cocktails Refashioned*, among many others, are indicative of the elite level at which women are now operating as professionals in this field.

JOURNALISTS AND COCKTAIL STORYTELLERS

As the craft cocktail movement picked up steam in the late aughts, the consumer thirst for cocktail-related content led some journalists to carve out niches for themselves as drinks and hospitality experts. Whether it was reporting on the opening of a new craft distillery, the launch of a new bar menu, or the history of a forgotten spirit, a number of notable women have made their name as translators of cocktail trends and the de facto bridge between the trade and consumers.

One of the most influential of these journalists has been Kara Newman. After first starting out covering the finance and economics of the food industry, her personal love of food and drink led her to switch focus to spirits and cocktails just as the craft cocktail movement was taking off. She has since contributed articles on the history and culture of the cocktail to such banner publications as the *New York Times*, the *Wall Street Journal*, the *Washington Post*, and the *Atlantic*, and in 2009, became the first woman to review spirits for a commercial publication when she was appointed spirits editor of *Wine Enthusiast* magazine.

One issue Kara noticed over the years as the cocktail was becoming a revered art form once again, was how it was simultaneously becoming less accessible to the home mixologist. The rare or esoteric ingredients and complicated techniques that bartenders were often using to create incredible hospitality experiences were leaving many home hosts out in the cold. As she watched her contemporary male journalists tie themselves up in knots over the precise techniques, formulae, and etymology that defined specific drinks, she saw the opportunity to sell the story as something much simpler.

From 2012 to 2019, Kara wrote prolifically about cocktails for the home audience, producing an average of one new book per year. Topics ranged from batched drinks in *Cocktails for a Crowd*; easy equal part recipes in the best-selling *Shake. Stir. Sip.*; to nighttime drinks, in the highly acclaimed *Nightcap*. Kara's books have received wide praise, and in 2013, her drinks journalism was recognized with an award from the highly prestigious International Association of Culinary Professionals (IACP). Other notable female journalists also produced award-winning cocktail books alongside Kara during this time, including the *Ultimate Bar Book*, by Mittie Helmich; *The 12 Bottle Bar*, by David and Lesley

Jacobs Solmonson; *Ten Cocktails*, by Alice Lascelles; and *The One-Bottle Cocktail*, by Maggie Hoffman. These works cleverly simplify the cocktail and make it approachable to a wide audience. In addition, such works as Emma Janzen's *Mezcal*, Talia Baiocchi and Leslie Pariseau's *Spritz*, and Rebekah Peppler's *Aperitif* explore new ways to make the cocktail relevant, thereby expanding the horizon of the category as a whole.

RAISING A GLASS TO FEMINISM

With the development of a fourth wave of feminism emerging around 2010, the focus of women and drinks has shifted once again. In this new phase, women have been taking on the stereotypes of women as drinkers, the inherent misogyny of the liquor world, and the very definition of gender as it relates to drinks. So strong has been the desire to reframe women's relationship with the cocktail, that between 2016 and 2018, more than half a dozen cocktail books connecting drinks to feminism and famous feminist figures were published.

In the first of the genre, Jeanette Hurt's *Drink Like a Woman: Shake, Stir, Conquer, Repeat* remixes classic cocktail recipes with prominent female mixologists and garnishes them with stories of iconic women from history. Drinks include feminist reinterpretations of classics, with names like Consensual Sex on the Beach, the Zeldapolitan, and the Bloody Mary Richards. In the introduction to the book, Jeanette argues against the myth of the "girly drink," stating, "There are no 'girly' drinks. There are no 'manly man' drinks. There are just *drinks*, and each human has their own preferences."

In a similar vein, in *Drinking Like Ladies*, Boston bartenders and writers Kirsten Amann and Misty Kalkoffen pose the rhetorical question, "What does it mean to drink like a lady?" In a backlash to negative stereotypes of women from previous eras of the cocktail, they reply, "To us, it's enjoying a well-balanced cocktail, passing on drinks that cover up the flavors of alcohol, learning about strong cocktails from strong-minded women, and never being pigeonholed into a 'skinny girl' cocktail." The book includes 75 cocktails from the world's leading female bartenders, with toasts to powerful women in history.

In Merrily Grashin's best-selling book *Women's Libation: Cocktails to Celebrate a Woman's Right to Booze*, classic cocktail recipes are given a feminist twist, with such drinks as the Rosé the Riveter Spritz and Sloe Gin-der Equality Negroni. Meanwhile, in *A Woman's Drink: Bold Recipes for Bold Women*, New York City bar owner and entrepreneur Natalka Burian provides an antidote to what she views as the elitist, inflexible, and overly masculine world of craft mixology. "No one should ever feel intimidated mixing, drinking, or even talking about cocktails," she writes, "whether it's a mansplaining suspendered bartender or a pompous uncle." Recipes in the book include elevated classics like the Tequila Old-Fashioned as well as modern mainstays like the Negroni and Aperol Spritz.

The message to the rest of the drinking world from each of these books is clear: when it comes to cocktails, women are more than capable of holding their own.

REWRITING COCKTAIL HISTORY

With a growing interest in the world of craft cocktails has come a growing interest in documenting their histories. One of the first people to write any kind of history of the cocktail was *Vogue* editor Jill Spalding, in her lavish coffee table book *Blithe Spirits*, published in 1988. In the book, she traces the origin of the cocktail in America from the stills of the Founding Fathers, through the bright young things of the 1920s, the golden age of Hollywood, and the glamour revival of the '80s. More recently, such journalists as the aforementioned Kara Newman and Jeanette Hurt have researched articles for the likes of *Forbes*, *Thrillist*, and *Wine Enthusiast* on historical topics ranging from the history of women bartending to the history of women and gin. Still many academic researchers have entered the fray producing numerous papers and dissertations on the history and politics of gender and drink.

One of the most respected female authorities on the history of spirits and the cocktail to emerge over the past few decades has been Anistatia Miller who, together with her partner, Jared Brown, has published or contributed to more than 30 books on the topic, including the best-selling book on the Martini, *Shaken Not Stirred*, and the definitive history of mixed drinks from 7000 BC to the 20th century, *Spirituous Journey: A History of Drink*. Anistatia's sweet spot as a researcher is her uncanny ability to debunk commonly held myths about cocktails. For example, she and Jared were the first to find the connection between Margaret Brown and the Bee's Knees cocktail, and they have also traced the etymology of many other well-known drinks, such as the Cosmopolitan, Bloody Mary, and Moscow Mule.

When it comes to African American culinary and drink history, there is no contemporary writer more influential than Toni Tipton Martin. In 2015, she published the groundbreaking culinary history book *The Jemima Code*, chronicling the contributions of men and women of African descent to the culture of food and drink in America and tracing their impact on the cuisine and hospitality of today. Presenting over 150 cookbooks with Black authors, from Malinda Russell, in the 19th century, to Bertha Turner and Freda De Knight, in the 20th, she has proven unequivocally the essential role that Black men and women have played in the story of the cocktail.

Drawing on the recipes from these books, in 2019 Toni published the award-winning recipe book *Jubilee*. In her chapter on beverages, she shares drink recipes from notable Black women authors, including Wine Punch, from Ruth Gaskins's *A Good Heart and a Light Hand*; Ice Milk Punch, from Ethel Dixon and Bibby Tate's *Colorful Louisiana Cuisine in Black and White*; and a John Toddy, from Rebecca West's *Rebecca's Cookbook*. *Jubilee* won Toni her second James Beard Award, as well as an IACP award, and was named a book of the year by National Public Radio, the *New York Times*, the *New Yorker*, the *Atlantic*, and the *Chicago Tribune*, among many others. At the time of writing, Toni is set to release a new book on the history of Black mixology, *Juke Joints, Jazz Clubs, and Juices*, featuring two centuries of cocktail recipes from such notable authors as Atholene Peyton.

Following in Toni's footsteps, in 2022, writer Tamika Hall joined forces with bartender Colin Asare-Appiah to publish *Black Mixcellence*, the first comprehensive guide to Black mixology in the United States. In the prologue to the book, Tamika reminds us that "Cocktails and spirits are all part of an industry that we, as African Americans, have played a major role in for years," and that "Like a lot of our contributions to the history of the country, credit wasn't given where credit was due." Through extensive research into the role of Black men and women in spirits production and bartending over the centuries, Tamika and Colin set the stage for a new generation of Black bartenders to make their mark on the cocktail. The book contains 75 modern recipes from some of the leading figures in the country, including Tiffanie Barriere, Camille Wilson, Joy Spence, and Madeline Maldonado.

Whereas the history of the cocktail has tended to focus on the work of male bartenders in a predominantly male world, these trailblazing women are uncovering new truths about the cocktail and actively writing women and other overlooked groups back into the story. The experience of the cocktail today—not only how one is made, but also what it *means* to have a cocktail—is all the richer for it.

CRAFT COCKTAILS

As bartenders, journalists, and researchers like Julie Reiner, Kara Newman, Anistatia Miller, and Tamika Hall have brought the craft of the cocktail home to a wide audience, Craft Hostesses have picked up the baton and run with it. Over the course of this period, women have reinvented their parlors as monuments to the cocktail. No longer relegated to the kitchen, the cocktail has regained pride of place in the living areas of the house once again. For the Craft Hostess, the cocktail is not just a social pastime, but an art form to be celebrated alongside other aspects of modern interior design, as such books as the 2017 *Art of the Bar Cart*, by Vanessa Dina, beautifully illustrate.

In many ways, the modern cocktail parlor is more nebulous than it once was. For the Craft Hostess, the space for drinking cocktails is not necessarily defined by one specific room anymore, but can be any place that simply *feels* right. It may even be virtual. Indeed, during the coronavirus pandemic that swept the globe at the very end of this period, all a good hostess needed to set up her cocktail parlor was a decent Wi-Fi connection and a working web camera.

One of the features of this period has not only been the rediscovery and renewed appreciation of lost drinks, but also an explosion in creativity and the invention of new drinks, some of which, like Audrey Saunders's Old Cuban, are already considered classics. Within the context of this broader explosion has been a deeper exploration of flavor and spirit profiles, and a widespread embrace of more challenging cocktail flavors and spirit ingredients such as amaro and mezcal. For the Craft Hostess in particular, the cocktail has been a tool for her to challenge her own palate, and in so doing, to challenge past stereotypes about women as drinkers.

In many ways, it's fair to say that the Negroni has been the poster child of the craft cocktail revival, especially as the movement has gone global, and it's interesting to observe how the drink features in some form or fashion in almost every cocktail book written by female authors during this period. Women like Julie Reiner have been influential in popularizing the drink, and her idea to infuse strawberries into a summer version of the cocktail as featured in *The Craft Cocktail Party* has been widely copied in bars all over the country.

Alongside the Negroni has been the rise of its close cousin, the Spritz, another cocktail that appears regularly in books by women of this era and has become a mainstay on bar menus everywhere during this time. The popularity of the Spritz in the United States has largely been driven by American consumers', especially women's, love of sparkling cocktails. Its bittersweet and bubbly flavor profile has made it an ideal brunch upgrade from the old-school Mimosa or Bellini, or a predinner alternative to the Champagne Cocktail or Kir Royale. If such Grand Hostesses as Perle Mesta, Elsa Maxwell, and Clara Walsh were hosting today, they would surely be serving the Spritz at their events.

Finally, the third cocktail to have received a real reawakening during the latest cocktail renaissance has been the Gin & Tonic. The British may have been enjoying their Gin & Tonics since the early 19th century, but the drink has been reaching new heights of fame since the early 2000s. And not only in Great Britain, either; the cocktail is now regularly featured on dedicated Gin & Tonic menus in bars and restaurants across the continents, from New York to Barcelona, Tokyo, and Sydney. The appeal of the modern Gin & Tonic to the new Craft Hostess lies as much in the adaptability of its presentation as it does in its original formula. Like hostesses of previous generations, women have been elevating the drink and making it their own through the application of creative garnishes and new flavors of tonic.

With their predinner roots, complex flavor profiles, and striking visual presentations, bitter cocktails have become staple serves on the menu of the Craft Hostess. And just as with prior cocktail trends, from the 1990s Tini to the 1890s Sherry Cobbler, women have been putting their own stamp on these drinks. A trend that we can now see has underpinned the way hostesses have brought the cocktail home for almost two centuries.

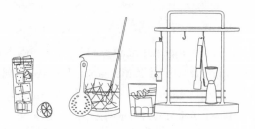

BITTER COCKTAILS

NEGRONI

Makes 1 cocktail

Despite the fact that the Negroni packs a strong flavor punch, its simplicity makes it surprisingly hard to screw up. The traditional recipe calls for equal parts gin, Campari, and sweet vermouth, but you can easily add more gin, try a different spirit, swap out the amaro, or use a combination of vermouths, and the end result almost always still works.

1 ounce gin
1 ounce Campari, amaro, or
   bitter liqueur

1 ounce sweet vermouth
Garnish: orange twist

Combine the gin, Campari, and sweet vermouth in a mixing glass and stir with ice until chilled. Strain into a double old-fashioned glass over a large cube of ice and twist the orange peel over the top of the drink. Alternatively, serve up in a cocktail glass.

+ *FLAVOR INSPIRATION:*
Try infusing strawberries into the Campari, for a twist on Julie Reiner's Summer Negroni, or replace the Campari with a blood orange amaro, for a fragrant Blood Orange Negroni. The popular Oaxacan Negroni, meanwhile, uses mezcal in place of gin.

BOULEVARDIER
Makes 1 cocktail

1 ounce bourbon or rye
1 ounce Campari, amaro, or
   bitter liqueur

1 ounce sweet vermouth
Garnish: maraschino cherry

Combine the bourbon, Campari, and sweet vermouth in a mixing glass and stir with ice until chilled. Strain into a chilled cocktail glass and garnish with the maraschino cherry.

WHITE NEGRONI
Makes 1 cocktail

1 ounce gin
1 ounce Suze or white
   gentian liqueur

1 ounce dry vermouth
Garnish: grapefruit twist

Combine the gin, Suze, and dry vermouth in a mixing glass and stir with ice until chilled. Strain into a chilled cocktail glass and twist the grapefruit peel over the drink before dropping it in.

VENETIAN SPRITZ

Makes 1 cocktail

The simple 3-2-1 formula for the Venetian Spritz is a rule that is oft recited. However, as journalists Talia Baiocchi and Leslie Pariseau tell us in their book Spritz, *it is a law that is not strictly policed. Rather, from watching bartenders make them day-in, day-out in Venice, they conclude, "the purest spritz is made by feel, gut instinct, and experimentation."*

3 ounces Prosecco
2 ounces Aperol, amaro, or
   bitter liqueur

1 ounce club soda
Garnishes: orange slice,
   green olive (optional)

Build the Prosecco, Aperol, and club soda, in order, over ice in a large wineglass. Garnish with the orange slice and an optional green olive.

+ *FLAVOR INSPIRATION:*

Changing or combining liqueurs will add new interest to this classic recipe. Try splitting the amaro with a grapefruit liqueur or grapefruit juice for a Grapefruit Spritz, or with a raspberry liqueur or Raspberry Syrup (page 37) for a Raspberry Spritz.

CLASSIC VARIATIONS

NEGRONI SBAGLIATO
Makes 1 cocktail

3 ounces Prosecco

1 ounce Campari, amaro, or
   bitter liqueur

1 ounce sweet vermouth

Garnish: orange slice

Build the prosecco, Campari, and vermouth, in order, over ice in a large wine glass. Garnish with the orange slice.

AMERICANO
Makes 1 cocktail

1½ ounces Campari, amaro,
   or bitter liqueur
1½ ounces sweet vermouth

3 ounces club soda

Garnish: orange slice

Fill a highball glass with ice. Pour in the Campari and vermouth, then fill with club soda. Garnish with the orange slice.

GIN & TONIC

Makes 1 cocktail

In Ten Cocktails, *the British journalist Alice Lascelles writes, "I've had a lot of poor drinks in my time, but there is still nothing that drives me quite as crazy as a badly made gin & tonic." The primary cause, she says, is not the gin or the tonic, but the ice. So, she instructs, "fill the glass all the way up and then, once the tonic is in, add another cube, two if possible, until the drink resembles a teetering glacier."*

1½ ounces gin	Garnish: lemon or
3 to 4 ounces tonic water	lime wedge

Fill a highball glass with ice, pour in the gin, and top up with tonic, adding more ice as the drink settles. Squeeze the citrus over the top of the drink before dropping it in among the ice.

✦ *FLAVOR INSPIRATION:*
Changing the garnish of the classic Gin & Tonic transforms the drink. Try alternative citrus, like grapefruit or blood orange; add fruits, such as sliced cucumbers or strawberries; provide a botanical flourish, with pink peppercorns or cardamom pods; or spike with fresh herbs, such as rosemary and thyme.

CLASSIC VARIATION

NO. 1 CUP

Makes 1 cocktail

½ ounce gin
½ ounce sweet vermouth
½ ounce Curaçao
   (page 42)

3 to 4 ounces tonic water or
   ginger ale
Garnishes: sliced cucumber,
   fresh strawberry, and
   lemon, plus a mint sprig

Fill a highball glass with ice; pour in the gin, vermouth, and Curaçao; and top up with the tonic or ginger ale. Garnish with slices of cucumber, strawberries, and lemon, pushing them down into the ice, and nestle the mint sprig into the top of the drink. Serve with a straw.

X

THE
RESPONSIBLE
HOSTESS

c. 2020–present

The hostess of today will be called upon to serve drinks in her home more than formerly, I imagine, and it were well to go back to the habits and customs of our grandmothers and be prepared to serve a refreshing drink in an attractive manner at a moment's notice.
—BERTHA STOCKBRIDGE, 1920

For as long as women have been writing about and serving cocktails, they have been writing about and serving nonalcoholic drinks, too. In fact, there are very few, if any, cocktail books written by women over the course of the last two centuries that do *not* address the importance of moderation or catering to the nondrinking guest. As we move through the third decade of the 21st century, a new generation of drinkers is increasingly sober and a new hostess is emerging who is experimenting with innovative low- and no-proof cocktails to meet the needs of this growing group of drinkers.

The Responsible Hostess has existed in one form or another across the generations and has understood that many of her guests may not be drinking or may want to limit their alcohol intake. She has responded by always serving cocktails in moderation and providing thoughtful alternatives. Today, the new generation of Responsible Hostess is building on the wisdom of the women who came before her, by leading a new movement in the cocktail that is bringing the entire genre full circle.

FROM TEMPERANCE TO RESPONSIBILITY

As the story of women and the cocktail has evolved, so too has their narrative around drinking and not drinking. For example, as you may recall of our earlier hostesses, Domestic Hostesses of the 19th century debated the social propriety of drinking, especially for women, and the need to create separate spaces for alcohol consumption. Then, in post-Prohibition America, after a decade of underground partying, Apartment Hostesses campaigned to set new standards for how cocktails should be served in the home, calling for moderation as the first rule to host by. In the midcentury, with debates around daytime drinking, Suburban Hostesses were concerned about the afternoon consumption of alcohol among bored suburban housewives and the three-martini lunches of their white-collar husbands.

By the late century, the problem of underage drinking and driving under the influence led to the National Minimum Drinking Age Act being passed in the United States, which raised the legal drinking age to 21 and made drunk driving illegal in all 50 states. For the Dinner Party Hostess, this led to an entirely new category of nondrinker in the room, the designated driver. Then, as the 20th century drew to a close, the attention of the City Hostess turned to health and wellness, the ingredients and caloric content of cocktails, and the impact of drinking on diet and fitness. Today, in the 2020s, social pressures on drinking and the marginalization of nondrinkers have made the question of social exclusion and personal choice a key topic of discussion for the new generation of Responsible Hostess.

Notwithstanding cultural changes, there have been many enduring reasons why someone may choose not to imbibe alcohol. These include such concerns as pregnancy and breastfeeding, medical issues, health problems, religious beliefs, drinking disorders, recovery, as well as simple personal choice. Today, under the banner of the sober-curious movement, people no longer feel compelled to give any reason at all for their decision not to drink. Indeed, surveys show that around one-third of adults of legal drinking age in the United States do not consume alcohol at all, a figure that has in fact remained consistent since the 1980s.

In short, nondrinking is not a new topic. The Responsible Hostess has existed in one form or another across the generations and has always understood that at least one in three of her guests may not be drinking any alcohol and that still more may want to limit their intake; therefore, serving alcohol in moderation and serving thoughtful no-proof cocktails has been an essential element of home hospitality from the start.

HOSTING IN MODERATION

Cocktail hour was originally called cocktail *hour* because it was intended to be a limited-time event, a precursor to something else. Consequently, early drink etiquette was never to serve more than two drinks during a one-hour cocktail event. The cocktails were also much smaller than today, the average pour being a jigger or one and a half ounces of base alcohol. At midcentury cocktail parties where events ran to two or more hours, hosts often described *decreasing* the size of the pour in their drinks as the evening went on, moving from something short and strong, such as a Martini or Old-Fashioned, at the beginning of the night to something longer—for instance, a Highball—toward the end. Lower-proof liquors, like sherry and sherry cocktails, were also commonly served.

The Prohibition period stands out as a time when women took the opportunity for a complete reset on the role of nonalcoholic beverages at their parties. When the Volstead Act came into force, not everyone took their liquor underground. Indeed, many women learned how to adapt their drinks with inventive techniques and ingredients that simulated the experience of a cocktail without the need for booze. Their tips, tricks, and recipes were published in widely read dry cocktail books, including *What to Drink*, by Bertha Stockbridge; *On Uncle Sam's Water Wagon*, by Helen Watkeys Moore; and *Prohibition Punches*, by Roxana Doran.

GOING TEA-TOTAL

One of the more influential women to write about no-proof cocktails during Prohibition was New York City fashion editor and cookbook author Bertha Stockbridge, who published *What to Drink*, her dry cocktail guide, in 1920. Bertha was already an expert on frugal cooking and housekeeping when she wrote the book, and she applied many of the same principles of wartime food restrictions to the new restrictions on alcohol. Her basic advice to the hostess was to look to her pantry, instead of her bar cart, to fix a delicious and satisfying drink.

One of the first ingredients that came to mind for Bertha was tea. Tea made sense because it was cheap, widely available, and already a common ingredient in the punches and cups that hostesses had served for long before Prohibition. Extolling the virtues of tea by quoting Chinese philosopher Chin Hung, she wrote, "Tea is better than wine, for it leadeth not to intoxication, neither does it cause a man to say foolish things. It is better than water, for it doth not carry disease, neither doth it act as poison."

There is evidence today to support the idea that tea could make a decent stand-in for spirits in zero-proof cocktails. First, teas contain the compounds l-theanine and caffeine, which stimulate the brain into releasing feelings of lucidity and contentedness, similar to the feeling of well-being that is triggered by the first few sips of alcohol. Second, teas contain polyphenols and tannins, which can mimic the texture of different spirits and create similar sensations on the tongue, from dry and astringent on the one hand, to soft and enveloping on the other. Finally, the many different varieties of tea, from white to green, black to herbal, cover a wide range of flavor profiles, each bringing its own subtlety and dimension to a drink.

SHRUBBING OFF THE BOOZE

In addition to teas, Bertha recognized that homemade shrubs and fruit vinegars, which had been made in the home for use in drinks for centuries, could be easily replicated for the Prohibition bar. As she wrote in *What to Drink*, "A generation or two ago every housewife who prided herself upon her ability as a hostess was very sure to have in her cellar shrubs and fruit vinegars of many kinds. For in this way she could always offer a guest a delightful and refreshing drink with the least amount of work and expenditure of time."

Today, fruit- and vegetable-based shrubs can function in a similar way to fruit or herbal liqueurs in cocktails by bringing sophistication, refreshment, and deep flavor to the zero-proof drink. This is because vinegar, as a fermented product, retains many of the same properties of alcohol. For example, vinegar is fat- and water-soluble, meaning it readily absorbs flavor compounds from organic matter immersed in it, making it a highly potent source of flavor in a cocktail. In addition, the acid content of the vinegar energizes taste buds and stimulates saliva production, causing sensations in the mouth that can feel similar to those produced by distilled spirits.

THE FRUIT OF ONE'S LABOR

In addition to shrubs, Domestic Hostesses have been making fruit and vegetable syrups in the home for generations as a way to preserve seasonal produce for use in cakes, desserts, medicines, and drinks. In *What to Drink*, Bertha's 30-plus syrups form the backbone of many of her dry cocktails, such as her homemade peach syrup in her Georgia Mint Julep recipe, or her apricot syrup in her Florida Sour.

Fruit syrups provide the essential sweet element to a cocktail that is either balanced out by a sour element, such as fresh citrus or the vinegar of a shrub, or a bitter element, such as tea, or botanical ingredients like bitters. In 1925, when the American cocktail trend was spreading across Europe, famous British herbalist Hilda Leyel wrote about the "newest American drinks" in a book on beverages called *Summer Drinks and Winter Cordials*. Although Britain was not under any form of prohibition at the time, Hilda nevertheless avoided the use of spirits in most of her recipes because she felt they were expensive and unnecessary to the pleasure of a drink, writing "Drinks, both alcoholic and non-alcoholic, if made with good materials need no apology."

Much like Bertha, Hilda relied on teas, vinegars, and fruit syrups to create the structure for her low- and no-proof cocktails, and leaned into her training as a botanist to create complex and unique flavor profiles. Noteworthy botanical recipes from her book include such drinks as Rose Mint Cup (grenadine, rose extract, and ginger ale), Tea Frappé (green tea, lemon juice, and mint), and Rhubarb and Raspberry Cup (raspberry vinegar, grated nutmeg, and crushed borage leaves).

GRAPE OR GRAIN, NEVER THE TWAIN

Beyond tea and shrubs, women have popularized other more readily available alcohol substitutes. For the lazy Prohibition-era Apartment Hostess, who might have had little to no interest in brewing tea, concocting syrups, or sourcing botanicals, the simplest way to replace the booze in her cocktails was to turn to the obvious fix, grape juice. In 1930, Roxana Doran, the wife of the former commissioner of Prohibition in the United States, published a book of grape juice cocktails titled *Prohibition Punches*. The recipes included contributions from many high-profile "drys" of the era, such as Ella Boole, president of the National Women's Christian Temperance Union; Laura Volstead Lomen, daughter of Andrew Volstead; and Mabel Walker Willebrandt, former assistant attorney general of the United States.

Naturally, given the status of the women involved, the book received a lot of attention in the press and the recipes were widely shared. Roxana's own signature recipe, called the 1930 Cocktail, was a mixture of grape juice, pineapple juice, lime juice, and ginger ale, garnished with mint and cucumber. In reviewing both the book and the cocktail, the *New York Times* compared it favorably to the real thing, concluding of the latter, "In the making it partially suggests a lime rickey, while it is served like a mint julep."

THE SOBER BOTANISTS

Such women as Bertha Stockbridge and Hilda Leyel were clearly a century ahead of their time with their ideas around the zero-proof cocktail. Sadly, however, after Repeal, efforts to create new or interesting booze-free homemade beverages mostly fell to the wayside. With the advent of mass consumerism, canned sodas, and ready-to-drink mixes in the mid-century, primary drink offerings for nondrinkers for around the next 50 years essentially became the redundant mixer options: club soda, cola, ginger ale, tomato juice, and the like.

It was not until the 2010s, when the craft cocktail revival was in full swing, that serious consideration was given once more to the virtues of the boozeless cocktail. Since this time, there has been an explosion in the number of alcohol-free wines, beers, and spirits on the market to make zero-proof drinks, as well as a wide array of gourmet mixers and ready-to-drink non-alcoholic cocktails. There has also been a renewed interest in mixing spirit-free cocktails from scratch.

Much like a century ago, the movement has been led by pioneering food writers, wellness-minded bartenders, and creative botanists. A number of women-authored books have built on the principles laid down by the likes of Bertha Stockbridge and Hilda Leyel, with botanical ingredients and simple homemade syrups and shrubs designed for the low- or no-alcohol cocktail-drinking enthusiast. These include the recently published works *The Low-Proof Happy Hour*, by Jules Aron; *Zero Proof*, by Maureen Petrosky; and *Free Spirit Cocktails*, by Camille Wilson.

Perhaps the most well-known botanist to influence the modern cocktail has been Amy Stewart. In 2013, she published the award-winning, internationally best-selling book *The Drunken Botanist*, in which she detailed more than 160 botanicals that play a role in the cocktail, through their use in the production of beers, wines, spirits, and liqueurs. Amy also wrote a guide to the easy cultivation of botanicals that could be useful cocktail ingredients, and many of these same items are arguably of interest to spirit-free cocktails, too. These include heating and cooling botanicals like ginger, pepper, and mint to create the bite in a drink; sour botanicals like raspberry, hibiscus, and pineapple, to provide astringency; and botanicals with high silica content, such as cucumber, watermelon, and aloe, to contribute mouth feel.

In her 2020 book *Good Drinks*, food editor Julia Bainbridge takes the art of the spirit-free cocktail to the next level, by showcasing 50 of the most advanced alcohol-free drink recipes made by the top bartenders in the United States today. While many of the drinks build on simple ideas for fruit syrups and teas, others are so involved in their sourcing and preparation that Julia considers them to be full "weekend projects," reserved for only the most serious and epicurious spirit-free host.

THE COCKTAIL IS IN THE EYE OF THE BEHOLDER

As we set out to mix zero-proof cocktails as elegant and satisfying as the real thing, it begs a return to the question, What is a cocktail anyway? Is it indeed a mix of spirits, bitters, sugar, and water as the traditional definition goes, or could we now take a more progressive view that a cocktail, whether with alcohol or without, is simply the act of hospitality in a glass?

In *Good Drinks*, Julia Bainbridge argues the case to dispense with such terms as *mocktail*, *zero-proof*, or *alcohol-free* cocktails, and simply to call all drinks, good drinks, as the title of her book suggests. As she writes, "Classic cocktail making is mainly about balancing flavors. The tension between sweet, sour, salty, bitter, and umami is what the palate wants in a drink, whether it contains alcohol or not."

It is also not only how the drink is mixed that matters, but how the glass is raised. Bertha Stockbridge wrote that "any drink is more pleasing to the palate if the eye is pleased," and her last piece of advice to the dry cocktail host was to focus as much on the presentation of the drink as what goes inside the glass. Quality glassware, a thoughtful garnish, a cozy corner of the parlor to gather, a toast—these are the elements that come together to create the ultimate cocktail experience, regardless of its level of proof.

The Responsible Hostess of the 21st century is bringing the story of the cocktail full circle as she drives the evolution of the cocktail in the present day. Two hundred years ago, when the very first cocktails were built on the cordials and ingredients that Domestic Hostesses made in their kitchens, women understood that the cocktail could not be separated from the wider system of home management. Today, the Responsible Hostess knows that the future of the low- and no-proof cocktail is not in what specific ingredients go together to make a particular drink, but in the broader role the ritual plays in the health and wellness of the family and the hospitality traditions of society as a whole.

RESPONSIBLE COCKTAILS

Lower-proof cocktails feature throughout many chapters of this book, including wine cups (e.g., the Champagne Cup, Claret Cup, Moselle Cup, Peach Sherbet, and Bishop); bitter cocktails (e.g., the Venetian Spritz and Americano); and sherry cocktails (e.g., the Sherry Cobbler and Sherry Blush). Many other cocktails can also be prepared with a half-spirit pour without negatively impacting the final drink; these include some tall mixed drinks (e.g., the Highball, Gin & Tonic, and Tom Collins), or fruit cocktails (e.g., the Screwdriver, Bloody Mary, and Piña Colada). Similarly, stirred cocktails (e.g., the Manhattan and Martini) can be "reversed," whereby the ratio of spirit to vermouth is swapped to lower the alcohol content of the drink without dramatically altering its flavor profile.

For zero-proof options, wines and spirits can be replaced with alcohol-free products in any recipe. Some cocktails, such as the Bloody Mary or Piña Colada, are sufficiently flavorful that they can be made without any liquor at all. Similarly, traditional drinks made with cocktail cordials (e.g., Lemonade, Pink Lemonade, and the Shrub Cocktail) are refreshing and sophisticated enough by themselves already.

In the recipes that follow, it feels appropriate to end by paying tribute to the last two centuries of the hostess in the cocktail parlor and reimagining a selection of classic drinks using homemade cordials and teas. From a functional perspective, as discussed, tea already shares some similar properties with spirits and with the breadth of options available can result in cocktails that are as delicious, complex, and satisfying as the real thing.

More important, from a social perspective, much like the act of mixing a cocktail, the ceremony of making tea is celebrated the world over as its own form of hospitality and is a ritual that has historically been led by women.

Since the very first cocktail parties originated in the parlors of the Tea

Party Hostess, it is fitting to now bring the story of the cocktail back to the place where it started. Henceforth, the 21st-century Cocktail Parlor can most appropriately be defined as the place where *all* hospitality in a glass is most cordially offered and received.

A Note on Brewing Tea for Cocktails

As any tea enthusiast will tell you, preparation is everything when it comes to brewing the perfect cup of tea, and so it should be when making tea for cocktails. As Bertha Stockbridge reminds us, "The labor and the time expended bring their own reward in the satisfaction gained by knowing that one has served a delicious drink delightfully made." Therefore, it is worth taking the time and care over this step.

The temperature of the water and the time the leaves are steeped make an enormous difference in the quality and taste of the end product. First, water should be freshly boiled for each brew, and the tea should always be steeped in a porcelain or china teapot, with the lid on to prevent heat loss during brewing. Once brewed, the tea can be strained and transferred to a glass jar or other container to cool. Never make or store brewed tea in a metal container, however, as the liquid will take on a metallic taste.

Second, as a general rule of thumb, 1 teaspoon of loose tea per every 8 ounces of water will make the ideal strength and solution for use in cocktails. Black and herbal teas are best steeped for 4 to 5 minutes in 205°F water, whereas green or white teas should be steeped for 2 to 3 minutes in 175°F water.

Finally, ideally tea should always be brewed for use the same day, although leftover cold tea can be stored for further use in the refrigerator for up to three days.

TEA COCKTAILS

TEA SOURS

In this tea version of the classic Bee's Knees cocktail, the earthy bergamot notes of a white Earl Grey tea make an elegant stand-in for gin. While in the Whiskey Tea Sour, the rich, smoky profile of lapsang souchong provides the depth of character needed to deputize for the whiskey. The use of bitters in either cocktail is optional but will add a further layer of botanical depth.

TEA'S KNEES
Makes 1 cocktail

2 ounces brewed white Earl
   Grey tea, cooled
¾ ounce fresh lemon juice
½ ounce Honey Syrup
   (page 37)

Dash of orange bitters
   (optional)
Garnish: lemon twist

Combine all the ingredients, except the lemon twist, with ice in a cocktail shaker, shake, then strain into a cocktail glass. Twist the lemon over the surface of the drink for aromatics and drop into the cocktail.

WHISTEA SOUR
Makes 1 cocktail

1 ounce egg white
  or aquafaba
2 ounces brewed lapsang
  souchong tea, cooled
¾ ounce fresh lemon juice

½ ounce Simple Syrup
  (page 36)
Dash of aromatic
  bitters (optional)
Garnish: maraschino cherry

First, dry shake the egg white or aquafaba by itself in a cocktail shaker until it is really foamy. Then, add the brewed tea, lemon juice, simple syrup, and bitters to the shaker, along with some ice, and shake hard. Place the maraschino cherry at the bottom of a cocktail glass and strain the cocktail over the top.

TEA DAISIES

In this tea-based Cosmopolitan, hibiscus tea complements the tartness of the cranberry while the triple sec is replaced with fresh orange juice, simple syrup, and the optional dash of orange bitters. In the tea-based Margarita, meanwhile, delicately scented jasmine green tea brings a sweet floral note in place of the traditional tequila.

COSMOPOLITEA
Makes 1 cocktail

2 ounces brewed hibiscus tea, cooled
½ ounce fresh orange juice
1 ounce cranberry juice
½ ounce fresh lime juice

¼ ounce Simple Syrup (page 36)
Dash of orange bitters (optional)
Garnish: lemon twist

Combine all the ingredients, except the lemon twist, with ice in a cocktail shaker, shake, then strain into a cocktail glass. Garnish with the lemon twist.

MARGARITEA
Makes 1 cocktail

2 ounces brewed jasmine green tea, cooled
½ ounce fresh orange juice
1 ounce fresh lime juice

½ ounce Simple Syrup (page 36)
Dash of orange bitters (optional)
Garnish: lime wheel

Combine all ingredients, except the lime wheel, with ice in a cocktail shaker, shake, then strain into a cocktail glass, or over fresh ice in a rocks glass. Garnish with the lime wheel.

TEA APERITIVI

The intense flavor of a homemade cherry shrub brings refreshment, sophistication, and a deep red hue to the zero-proof aperitif cocktail, while the use of chai tea adds a layer of spice. The additions of tonic and grapefruit juice round out the bitter-sweet profile in each of these spirit-free predinner drinks.

AMERICA-NO
Makes 1 cocktail

1½ ounces brewed chai
tea, cooled
½ ounce Cherry Shrub
(page 41)

Dash of aromatic
bitters (optional)
3 to 4 ounces tonic
Garnish: orange slice

Pour the chai tea, shrub, and bitters, in order, into a highball glass or wineglass filled with ice. Top with the tonic and garnish with the orange slice.

NO-GRONI
Makes 1 cocktail

1½ ounces brewed chai
tea, cooled
½ ounce Cherry Shrub
(page 41)

1 ounce grapefruit juice
Dash of aromatic
bitters (optional)
Garnish: orange slice

Pour the chai tea, shrub, grapefruit juice, and bitters, in order, into a rocks glass filled with ice and stir. Garnish with the orange slice.

TEA HIGHBALLS

Although these spritzy tea highballs don't contain alcohol, they are just as lovely when sipped poolside or on a sunny spring patio. The chamomile tea used in the Tea Spritzer has a dry and delicately floral flavor profile that is reminiscent of white wine, while mint tea enriched with homemade mint syrup is naturally the perfect fit for a Tea Mojito.

TEA SPRITZER

Makes 1 cocktail

2 ounces brewed chamomile
tea, cooled
½ ounce fresh lemon juice
¼ ounce Simple Syrup
(page 36)

3 to 4 ounces club soda
Garnishes: cucumber slices
and lemon wheels

Combine the tea, lemon juice, and simple syrup in a cocktail shaker filled with ice. Shake and strain over fresh ice in a highball glass or wineglass. Top with club soda and garnish with the cucumber and lemon slices.

TEA MOJITO

Makes 1 cocktail

2 ounces brewed mint
tea, cooled
½ ounce fresh lime juice
¼ ounce Mint Syrup (page 38)

3 to 4 ounces club soda
Garnishes: fresh mint and
lime wheels

Combine the tea, lime juice, and simple syrup in a cocktail shaker filled with ice. Shake and strain over fresh ice in a highball glass or wineglass. Top with club soda and garnish with the mint and lime wheels.

THE TOAST

Here's to the girl that's strictly in it,
Who doesn't lose her head, even for a minute,
Plays well the game and knows the limit
And still she gets all the fun there's in it
—JANET MADDISON, 1908

J ust like the wave of a hand is the universal sign for hello or good-bye, the raise of a glass is recognizable the world over as a symbol of good cheer. Toasting dates back to the very beginning of drinking, and over the centuries it has been traditional to toast to all kinds of figures from the gods, to national heroes, to absent friends, or simply to one another.

However, etiquette guides reveal that around the turn of the last century, it was customary after a dinner to have a toast that was specifically dedicated "To the Ladies." In 1904, hosting and etiquette writer Christine Herrick wrote that "toasts to women are most popular wherever conviviality prevails" and that whoever was nominated to deliver this ladies' tribute considered it "an honor which cannot be too highly esteemed."

In 1908, just as women were stepping out from their tea parlors into their cocktail parlors, such books as *Toasts You Ought to Know*, by writer Janet Maddison, revealed how much fun they were having with their newfound sense of freedom. Her toast to a woman who keeps her cool while going simultaneously all in on the action is surely as energizing to women today as it was a century ago.

Still today, the toast is arguably the most important prelude to a cocktail. A toast marks the significance not simply of an occasion, but of the people who gather to commemorate it. It gives meaning to a cocktail. And while the act of toasting feels like a reflex, there is an art to the way we raise our glass.

So, building on the advice of generations of convivial hostesses who came before us, I leave you with the Cocktail Parlor guide to delivering the perfect toast.

1. STAND AND DELIVER

You may have noticed that raising a toast is a little bit like parting the Dead Sea. As you stand up from your chair, clear your throat, and raise your glass, the folks around you are subconsciously triggered to pause in their tracks. The music somehow stops. You have about 10 seconds to begin delivering before people grow suspicious of your sudden exhibitionism.

2. RAISE YOUR GLASS

Now that you're standing with your glass held high, it is important that you keep it there. Both your elevated height and the raised stemware are a metaphor for the spirits you intend to lift with your words (and, if you watch, there is a direct correlation between the loftiness of your glass and how closely people pay attention).

3. A TOAST TO ALL

A toast, by definition, is inclusive. It includes people who are in the room and those who are not present. It includes the old and the young. It is not uncommon for it to include those who have passed and those who are still to be born. Don't leave anyone out, and make sure everyone has in their hand a glass that is full.

4. SHORT AND SWEET

Toasts can be long, toasts can be short,
Toasts can be funny and make people snort.
Toasts can rhyme, and oftentimes not.
Thirty seconds or less is what hits the spot.

5. RAISE SPIRITS

A toast is not a time to lament, criticize, or judge. It's certainly not a time to make jokes about others. You know what your mother used to say: if you don't have something nice to say, then certainly don't toast about it. Use your toast to lift the spirits of everyone in the room.

6. THE TOAST WORD

When your glass is raised you may notice your audience is held in a trancelike state. It is impossible for them to eat, drink, talk, or move. To release them from this spell, you must close with a safe word—*cheers, salud, cin-cin, prost,* or *bottoms-up* will usually do the trick.

7. KEEP EYES LOCKED

In certain parts of the world, locking eyes with the person you are toasting is the most sacred element of the toast. Without making eye contact at the crucial moment, the sentiment is considered insincere, undermining the connective power of the toast, and worse, potentially bringing on years of bad juju. Don't let their eyes get away!

8. CLINK BEFORE YOU DRINK

After making eye contact, it's time to connect glasses. Of course, in a crowded room this can always be a hand signal and a nod, but is there any sound sweeter than the symphonious ring of crystal on crystal?

9. YOU BEFORE ME

Remember that a toast is really about other people. Frankly, it's a little weird and self-indulgent to raise a glass to yourself. If you are the object of the toast, simply accept the compliment like a stoic old aunt and, if you wish, return the favor by passing it on to someone else.

10. NEVER REFUSE A TOAST

Finally, while it's acceptable to toast with an empty glass if you so choose, it's considered most churlish to refuse a toast altogether. Pity on the person who cannot accept the good wishes of others.

Cheers!

EPILOGUE

Back in 2015, when I had the idea to start a spirits company that would celebrate the role of women in gin, I decided I first needed to research the broader history of women and the cocktail. In the beginning, it seemed that there were going to be very few resources available for the task; however, I had no idea of the Pandora's box I was about to open! By now I must have read hundreds of thousands of words written by women about the cocktail over the past two centuries, and diving deeper into their life stories during the research for this book, I have found myself greatly inspired by every single one of them.

It's surely a universal truth that to be called a great host is one of the highest compliments one could hope to receive in one's life. However, to be hosted by a great host is surely one of life's greatest pleasures. And what I would give to be hosted by any one of the women in this book!

For a long time as I was writing this book, I thought about what I would serve in my own cocktail parlor if I had the honor of hosting one of these women today. I concluded that to pay tribute to any of these women properly, it would have to be something that is highly celebratory, unequivocally delicious, and uniquely personal to me.

So, if you'd care to join me for one final toast, I'd like to raise a glass to the women of the Cocktail Parlor with my own signature drink: the Pomp & Whimsy Spritz made with Champagne, grapefruit juice, and Pomp & Whimsy Gin Liqueur—an organic, cordial-style gin that is crafted from lychee, cucumber, orange, grapefruit, raspberry, jasmine, and other botanical lovelies, and is inspired by gins that were popular back when the spirit was better known as "Mother Gin."

To all the other hostesses out there, I hope you enjoy sipping *my* cordial as much as I enjoyed making it.

POMP & WHIMSY SPRITZ
Makes 2 cocktails

3 ounces Pomp & Whimsy
    Gin Liqueur
2 ounces pink
    grapefruit juice

6 ounces chilled Champagne
Garnish: grapefruit twist

First fill two wineglasses with ice. Combine the Pomp & Whimsy Gin Liqueur and grapefruit juice in a shaker, add ice to the shaker, and shake to chill. Strain equally into the two ice-filled wineglasses and top each with the Champagne. Garnish with the grapefruit twist.

BIBLIOGRAPHY

Looking to start your own library of cocktail books by women? Here are 100 or so sources referenced throughout the chapters of this book to help get you started.

Acton, Eliza. *Modern Cookery for Private Families*. Second edition revised and prepared for American housekeepers by Mrs. S. J. Hale. Lea and Blanchard, 1845.

Adams, Charlotte. *Home Entertaining: A Complete Guide*. Crown Publishers Inc., 1950.

Allen, Lucy G. *Table Service*. Little, Brown & Company, 1915.

Amann, Kirsten, and Misty Kalkoffen. *Drinking Like Ladies*. Quarry Books, 2018.

Aron, Jules. *The Low-Proof Happy Hour*. The Countryman Press, 2021.

Bainbridge, Julia. *Good Drinks*. Ten Speed Press, 2020.

Baiocchi, Talia, and Leslie Pariseau. *Spritz: Italy's Most Iconic Aperitivo Cocktail, with Recipes*. Ten Speed Press, 2016.

Baroni, Allana. *Flirtini*. Clarkson Potter, 2003.

Beeton, Isabella. *The Book of Household Management*. S. O. Beeton Publishing, 1861.

Beland, Nicole. *The Cocktail Jungle: A Girl's Field Guide to Shaking and Stirring*. Running Press, 2003.

Berk, Sally Ann. *The Martini Book: The First, the Last, the Only True Cocktail*. Black Dog & Leventhal, 1997.

Bradly, Mrs. Alexander Orr. *Beverages and Sandwiches for Your Husband's Friends*. Brentano's, 1893.

Brenner, Leslie. *Art of the Cocktail Party: The Complete Guide to Sophisticated Entertaining*. Plume, 1994.

Brooks, Karen, Gideon Bosker, and Reed Darmon. *Highballs High Heels: A Girl's Guide to the Art of Cocktails*. Chronicle Books, 2001.

Brown, Helen Evans, and Philip S. Brown. *A Book of Appetizers with a Number of Drinks*. The Ward Ritchie Press, 1958.

Bryan, Lettice. *The Kentucky Housewife*. Shepard & Stearns, 1839.

Burian, Natalka, and Scott Schneider. *A Woman's Drink*. Chronicle Books, 2018.

Bykofsky, Sheree, and Megan Buckley. *Sexy City Cocktails*. Adams Media, 2003.

Charming, Cheryl. *Frozen Drinks: An A to Z Guide to All Your Frozen Favorites*. Adams Media, 2008.

Child, Julia. *Julia Child & Company*. Alfred A. Knopf, 1978.

Coggins, Carolyn. *Successful Entertaining at Home*. Prentice-Hall, 1952.

Corson, Juliet. *Miss Corson's Practical American Cookery and Household Management*. Dodd, Mead & Company, 1885.

Daly, Maureen. *The Perfect Hostess*. Dodd, Mead & Company, 1950.

Daughters of the American Revolution. *A Book of Beverages by the Colonel Timothy Bigelow Chapter*. The Merrymount Press, 1904.

David, Natasha. *Drink Lightly*. Clarkson Potter, 2022.

De Knight, Freda. *A Date with a Dish*. Johnson Publishing Company Inc., 1948.

De Salis, Harriet. *Drinks à la Mode*. Longmans, Greene & Company, 1891.

Dina, Vanessa. *The Art of the Bar Cart*. Chronicle Books, 2017.

Dixon, Ethel, and Bibby Tate. *Colorful Louisiana Cuisine in Black and White*. Pelican Publishing, 1988.

Doran, Roxana B. *Prohibition Punches*. Dorrance & Company, Inc., 1930.

Draper, Dorothy. *Entertaining Is Fun! How to Be a Popular Hostess*. Doubleday, Doran & Company, Inc., 1941.

Elliott, Virginia, and Phil Strong. *Shake 'Em Up! A Practical Handbook of Polite Drinking*. Brewer & Warren, Inc., 1930.

Farmer, Fannie, ed. *The Woman's Dictionary and Encyclopedia: Everything a Woman Wants to Know*. The Anderson Publishing Company, 1909.

Flexner, Marion W. *Cocktail-Supper Cookbook*. Bramhall House, 1955.

Foley, Jaclyn Wilson. *The Pink Drink Book*. Foley Books, 2003.

Frankel, Bethenny. *Skinnygirl Cocktails*. Atria Books, 2014.

Ganseth, Sandra, ed. *Better Homes and Gardens Casual Entertaining Cook Book*. Meredith Corporation, 1981.

Gaskins, Ruth. *A Good Heart and a Light Hand*. Simon & Schuster, 1970.

Gill, Martha. *Modern Cocktails & Appetizers*. Longstreet Press, 1998.

Gillette, Fanny Lemira, and Hugo Ziemann. *The Whitehouse Cookbook: A Comprehensive Cyclopedia of Information for the Home*. The Werner Company, 1887.

Glasse, Hannah. *The Art of Cookery, Made Plain and Easy*. Printed by the author. 1747.

Glover, Ellye Howell. *"Dame Curtsey's" Book of Salads, Sandwiches and Beverages*. A. C. McClurg & Co., 1916.

Godsell, Patricia. *The Diary of Jane Ellice*. Oberon Press, 1975.

Grashin, Merrily. *Women's Libation*. Plume, 2017.

Hale, Sarah. *The Good Housekeeper, or The Way to Live Well and to Be Well While We Live*. Weeks, Jordan & Company, 1839.

Hall, Tamika. and Colin Asare-Appiah. *Black Mixcellence: A Comprehensive Guide to Black Mixology.* Kingston Imperial, 2022.

Heaton, Rose Henniker. *The Perfect Hostess.* E. P. Dutton & Co., Inc., 1931.

Helmich, Mittie. *Ultimate Bar Book.* Chronicle Books, 2006.

Henderson, Mary. *Practical Cooking and Dinner Giving.* Harper & Brothers, 1877.

Herrick, Christine, and Marion Harland. *Consolidated Library of Household Cooking and Modern Recipes.* Higgins & Seiter, 1904.

Hess, Karen. *Martha Washington's Booke of Cookery.* Columbia University Press, 1981.

Hillis, Marjorie. *Live Alone and Like It: A Guide for the Extra Woman.* Bobbs-Merrill Company, 1936,

Hoffman, Maggie. *The One-Bottle Cocktail.* Ten Speed Press, 2018.

Huerta, Alba, and Marah Stets. *Julep: Southern Cocktails Refashioned.* Lorena Jones Books, 2018.

Hurt, Jeanette. *Drink Like a Woman.* Seal Press, 2016.

Janzen, Emma. *Mezcal: The History, Craft & Cocktails of the World's Ultimate Artisanal Spirit.* Voyageur Press, 2017.

Judson, Helena. *Light Entertaining; A Book of Dainty Recipes for Special Occasions.* Butterick Publishing Company, 1910.

Kingsland, Mrs. Florence Burton. *Etiquette for All Occasions.* Doubleday, 1901.

Lascelles, Alice. *Ten Cocktails.* Saltyard, 2015.

Leslie, Eliza. *Directions for Cookery, in Its Various Branches.* Carey & Hart, 1837.

Leyel, Mrs. C. F. *Summer Drinks and Winter Cordials.* George Routledge & Sons Ltd., 1925.

London, Anne, and Robert London. *Cocktails and Snacks.* World Publishing Company, 1953.

Madison, Janet. *Toasts You Ought to Know.* Reilly & Britton Company, 1908.

Maxwell, Elsa. *How to Do It: Or the Lively Art of Entertaining.* Little, Brown & Company, 1957.

Mesta, Perle. *Perle, My Story.* McGraw-Hill Book Company, Inc., 1960.

Miller, Anistatia R., and Jared M. Brown. *Shaken Not Stirred: A Celebration of the Martini.* HarperCollins, 1997.

Mix, Ivy. *Spirits of Latin America.* Ten Speed Press, 2020.

Momosé, Julia, and Emma Janzen. *The Way of the Cocktail: Japanese Traditions, Techniques, and Recipes.* Clarkson Potter, 2021.

Moore, Helen Watkeys. *On Uncle Sam's Water Wagon; 500 Recipes for Delicious Drinks, Which Can Be Made at Home.* G. P. Putnam Sons, 1919.

Moritz, Mrs. Charles F., and Adèle Kahn. *The Twentieth Century Cookbook.* G. W. Dillingham Co., 1898.

Mustipher, Shannon. *Tiki: Modern Tropical Cocktails.* Rizzoli, 2019.

Newman, Kara. *Shake. Stir. Sip.* Chronicle Books, 2016.

Peppler, Rebekah. *Aperitif.* Clarkson Potter, 2018.

Petrosky, Maureen. *Zero Proof.* Robert Rose, 2021.

Peyton, Atholene. *The Peytonia Cook Book.* Marshall Publishing Company, 1906.

Phillips, Amy Lyman. *A Bachelors Cupboard: Containing Crumbs Culled from the Cupboards of the Great Unwedded.* John W. Luce & Company, 1906.

Randolph, Mary. *The Virginia Housewife: Or, Methodical Cook.* Davis & Force, 1824.

Reiner, Julie, and Kaitlyn Goalen. *The Craft Cocktail Party.* Grand Central Life & Style, 2015.

Rodnitzky, Donna Pliner. *Tipsy Smoothies.* Clarkson Potter, 2003.

Russell, Malinda. *A Domestic Cookbook: Containing a Careful Selection of Useful Receipts.* Printed by the author, 1866.

Rutledge, Sarah. *The Carolina Housewife.* W. R. Babcock, 1847.

Schur, Sylvia. *Seagram's Complete Party Guide: How to Succeed at Party Planning, Drink Mixing, the Art of Hospitality.* Warner Books, 1979.

Sherwood, Mary E. *Manners and Social Usages.* Harper & Brothers, 1884.

Smith, Barbara. *Entertaining and Cooking for Friends.* Artisan, 1995.

Solmonson, David, and Lesley Jacobs Solmonson. *The 12 Bottle Bar.* Workman Publishing Company, 2014.

Southworth, May E. *One Hundred and One Beverages.* Paul Elder & Company, 1904.

Spalding, Jill. *Blithe Spirits.* A. Rosenbaum Projects, 1988.

Stegner, Mabel. *Electric Blender Recipes.* Gramercy Publishing Company, 1952.

Stewart, Amy. *The Drunken Botanist.* Algonquin Books, 2013.

Stewart, Martha. *Entertaining.* Clarkson Potter, 1982.

Stockbridge, Bertha E. L. *What to Drink.* D. Appleton & Company, 1920.

Tipton-Martin, Toni. *Jubilee.* Clarkson Potter, 2019.

Toye, Nina, and Alec Henry Adair. *Drinks Long & Short.* William Heinemann Ltd., 1925.

Tsutsumi, Cheryl Chee. *101 Great Tropical Drinks.* Island Heritage, 2003.

Turner, Bertha L. *The Federation Cook Book: A Collection of Tested Recipes Contributed by the Colored Women of the State of California.* Pasadena, 1910.

Tyree, Marion Cabell. *Housekeeping in Old Virginia Containing Contributions from 250 of Virginia's Noted Housewives.* John P. Morton & Company, 1879.

West, Rebecca. *Rebecca's Cookbook.* Printed by the author, 1942.

Whitaker, Alma. *Bacchus Behave! The Lost Art of Polite Drinking.* Frederick A. Stokes Company, 1933.

Williams, Florence. *Dainties for Home Parties: A Cook-Book for Dance Suppers, Bridge Parties, Receptions, Luncheons and Other Entertainments.* Harper & Brothers, 1915.

Wilson, Camille. *Free Spirit Cocktails.* Chronicle Books, 2022.

Wisner, Penelope. *Summer Cocktails.* Chronicle Books, 1999.

Woodman, Mary. *Cocktails, Ices, Sundaes, Jellies and American Drinks: How to Make Them.* W. Foulsham & Co. Ltd., 1929.

Woolley, Hannah. *The Queen-Like Closet.* Richard Lowndes, 1670.

ACKNOWLEDGMENTS

Thank you to all the friends, colleagues, and supporters who have been a part of this journey. To Robert Simonson, for being the first to recognize there was a story here; Joelle Delbourgo, who persuaded me it could be a book; and Isabel McCarthy and the team at Countryman Press, who understood the vision right away.

Thank you to T.J. River for the creative work that makes every day feel like Christmas. To my past and present teammates and mentors at Pomp & Whimsy—Vanessa Urian, Nori de a Cruz, Todd Gallopo, Kendra Underwood, Jaron Berkhemer, Colin Baugh, Cindy Gallop, Cate Luzio, and the late Ted Roman—who have pushed me to follow my instincts and endured my many hours of raving on this topic.

I am indebted to the prior works of Robert, as well as David Wondrich, Catherine Murdock, Toni Tipton Martin, Anistatia Miller, Jared Brown, Jeanette Hurt, Mallory O'Meara, Camper English, and many other researchers and writers, without whom this project would surely have taken many more years to finish. To Linda Pelaccio, Kara Newman, Greg Benson, Sother Teague, Damon Boelte, Noah Rothbaum, Meaghan Dorman, Lynnette Marrero, Frank Caiafa, and Erick Castro, who each so generously shared their platforms to give voice to early versions of this story.

I am deeply grateful to the authors who gave up their time to share their work with me, including Anistatia, Kara, and Jeanette, as well as Amy Stewart, Nicole Zeman, Tamika Hall, Jules Aron, and Julie Reiner. Thank you also to Jeanne Mockard for sharing your beautiful memories of your dear friend, Julia Child, with me.

Finally, I am thankful for the people and institutions that helped shape me long before I knew I was ever going to embark on this project. To the high school careers adviser who predicted I would become either an accountant or a librarian. I became neither, but I did write a book about books. To Somerville College, University of Oxford, which I believe has turned out more inspiring women than any other institution in the world. And of course, to my parents, Nigel and Marilyn, and my brother and sister-in-law, Robin and Emily, the true writers in the family.

And to Todd, Theo, and Annabel, for always keeping my cup full.

INDEX

Recipes are indicated in **bold**.